mobile
MARKETING

Also by Matt Haig...

The B2B E-Commerce Handbook:
How to Transform Your Business-to-business Global Marketing Strategy
Designed to show every online company how to use the Net as a key marketing tool, full of advice on everything regarding B2B marketing, including a directory and glossary.

E-Business Essentials
Published in association with The Sunday Times
Nobody can afford to ignore the impact of the Internet on business; a Web site is no longer an optional extra. *E-Business Essentials* provides you with the knowledge necessary to make a success of your e-business activity, whether purely online or as support to your offline business.

E-Mail Essentials:
How to Make the Most of E-communication
Although e-mail is the most frequently used Internet application, many people are uncertain about how to use it effectively. By following Matt Haig's advice, you will have the confidence and enthusiasm to benefit fully from this all too often underestimated business tool.

The E-Marketing Handbook:
An Indispensable Guide to Marketing Your Products and Services on the Internet
The E-Marketing Handbook will take you step-by-step through the process of developing and implementing an e-marketing plan. Every aspect is covered in detail and organized so that you can dip in and out if you wish or follow the advice in a logical fashion, and there's also lots of examples and cases, recommended sites for further help and a very useful e-marketing dictionary.

E-PR:
The Essential Guide to Public Relations on the Internet
'Refreshingly devoid of the hysterical e-branding waffle that can be found in many other tomes about the Internet... a good solid book.'
Marketing Week
'A useful introduction to the strange and new world of E-PR.'
e-volve

If You're So Brilliant... How Come You Don't Have an E-Strategy?:
The Essential Guide to Online Business
In spite of the recent dot.com boom and bust, e-commerce is thriving like never before. This book gives you a crash course in everything you need to know and do to ensure success.

Published by Kogan Page and available from all good bookshops. For further information, please contact the publishers at the following address:

Kogan Page
120 Pentonville Road
London N1 9JN
Tel: 020 7278 0433
Fax: 020 7837 6348
www.kogan-page.co.uk

mobile MARKETING

THE MESSAGE REVOLUTION

MATT HAIG

KOGAN
PAGE

First published in 2002

Kogan Page Limited
120 Pentonville Road
London N1 9JN
UK

Kogan Page US
22 Broad Street
Milford CT 06460
USA

British Library Cataloguing in Publication Data

A CIP record for this book is available from the British Library.

ISBN 0 7494 3798 7

Typeset by Jean Cussons Typesetting, Diss, Norfolk
Printed and bound in Great Britain by Biddles Ltd, Guildford and King's Lynn
www.biddles.co.uk

Contents

Figures

Foreword

Picture this. An energy drink wants to cement its image as a sports-performance beverage. It prints a mobile number on every can, inviting consumers to play a sports trivia game with three friends. Each player receives a text message with the same question at the same time, and the fastest correct response wins. Then, with the player's permission, the drink keeps in touch with regular mobile vouchers, breaking sports news, updates on local events, and polls on popular culture. Periodically it runs 'viral' promotions to further build its database. Not only has the company created an iron link with its young, sports-related image, but it has also established a one-to-one relationship with its consumers – all for the price of a single television commercial.

This is the reality of mobile marketing. Mobile phones are always with us; they are the most personal device we own. They are also targetable individually, and interactive. Moreover, reaching people through them can cost a tenth of the price of a postage stamp. In retrospect, it seems odd that marketing to mobile phones only really took off in 2001.

It was not always this way. When I first started looking at mobile marketing in 1999, on behalf of Psion Computers, the conventional wisdom was that banner ads on WAP mobile Internet pages, and occasionally on peer-to-peer text messages, would dominate. This was the equivalent of the first television ads featuring attractive women walking across a stage holding a billboard. We couldn't see beyond the Internet.

Mobile Marketing helps us to widen our perception. In fact, as Matt Haig explains, mobile marketing is an entirely unique medium.

Brands first rushed to mobile in order to communicate with youths in a manner relevant to them. Quickly, even staid firms embraced mobile as direct marketing with a difference. Imagine a letter that was always opened as soon as it went through the mail slot, allowing an instant response, and delivered for pennies. The potential is huge.

The dangers are just as apparent. Mobiles can be uniquely intrusive. Moreover, network operators must know where the mobile is in order for it to work. The scenario of receiving ads from every store you walk past isn't only commercially infeasible – it's frightening.

Fortunately the industry has learnt from e-mail marketing, where spam tarnished the reputation of the entire industry and depressed response rates from legitimate opt-in approaches. Quickly, standards were adopted worldwide specifying that mobile was inherently different. Consumers must give prior consent to receiving marketing messages, and it must always be easy to opt out of further communication. These guidelines are echoed throughout *Mobile Marketing*. The economics of sending spam can be compelling, but by turning advertisers and consumers firmly against it, as well as enforcing strict industry regulations, the problem has so far remained largely contained.

The coming years will see massive innovation, as the chapter on 'Future technologies' observes. The advent of colour screens, always-on high-speed connections, and streaming video is creating exciting possibilities. Mobiles will never be a substitute for television. They have already shown that they can offer something entirely different. Something which, potentially at least, can be even more powerful than traditional forms of media. They can extend the meaning of a brand from an image into a lifestyle.

As this book recognizes, the pace of innovation in mobile marketing is relentless. Last quarter's breakthrough campaign quickly becomes ho-hum. But the power of the medium is vast to explore and will remain with us in whatever form the future may offer.

Steve Wunker
CEO, Brainstorm Marketing
UK Director, Mobile Marketing Association

Introduction

Let's start with the bad news. After years of trying to impress consumers with spectacular advertising campaigns packed with mindblowing special effects and production values Spielberg himself would be proud of, we find out the truth. When it comes to marketing campaigns, consumers are minimalists.

This shocking fact emerged at the turn of the millennium, when consumers actually started to ask for their marketing messages. They picked up their mobile phones, dialled a number, and requested text messages from companies.

That's right. A small grey band of text, limited to 160 characters, proved to be as, if not more, effective than the most expensive television ad or the widest billboard you can imagine. Moreover, not only have people asked to receive them, but they also said they were willing to pay for them.

Of course, if we can swallow our collective pride, this is in actual fact the good news. Traditional media is as important as it ever was, but its power can be intensified by integrating it with this new form of marketing. Indeed the mobile phone, and text messaging in particular, have completely changed the whole marketing process. In this new context, consumers now notify companies when they want to sign up to a campaign. The challenge lies in making sure they want to receive messages in the first place. Marketers also need to respect the consumer's right to choose, as uninvited mobile 'spam' has proved even more unwelcome than its e-mail counterpart. After all, a mobile phone is a uniquely personal device, primarily used for communicating with friends. Any company entering this personal space without an invite is, quite frankly, asking for trouble.

Reaping the rewards

For those companies that have already made the effort to attract mobile users, the rewards have been great. The club kids of Ibiza, who (as we shall see) were some of the first targets of mobile marketing campaigns, have proved remarkably loyal to the brands who sent them messages. Even Coca-Cola, the champion of multi-million dollar global television campaigns, have pulled back on television advertising in some countries to concentrate on text messaging. Very few who have entered the mobile marketing arena have left disappointed. Furthermore, although text messaging via SMS (the short messaging service) originated as a teen trend, it has now gained mainstream appeal. Indeed, banks, car insurers and television stations have all used mobile marketing campaigns to build relations with older mobile users.

Predictably, many are still sceptical. They have seen enough new media bandwagons come and go, to stand back and watch this one pass them by. The difference here, however, is that the hype has arrived after the technology has proved itself. Okay, so the mobile Internet has yet to fulfil its promise (the signs are looking better all the time), but text messaging was originally the most unhyped of all new technologies. Indeed, operators did not even bother to include instructions regarding how it should be used when it first appeared.

Yet despite its low-key arrival, SMS has grown rapidly in popularity. Furthermore, despite the relatively limited amount of commercial services available, mobile users are requesting alerts and other SMS services in huge numbers.

Carried out responsibly, mobile marketing provides a way of breaking through the media clutter to communicate in the most direct and powerful way with your target audience customers on their own terms.

About this book

The aim of this book is to provide an overview of the whole mobile marketing arena, with a particular focus on how it has changed the way businesses of every size can get their message across to customers. Rather than simply offer general guidelines, I have tried where possible to support any principles with examples of real campaigns.

In short, this book will help you:

- realize the most powerful marketing weapon is in your pocket;
- understand the different ways people and companies use mobile technology;
- spread a marketing 'virus';
- integrate a text message campaign with your other marketing activity;
- harness the power of text messaging to convert mobile users into customers;
- ask for permission (and get it);
- avoid message fatigue;
- get to grips with generation text;
- appreciate the variety of campaigns on offer;
- translate mobile jargon;
- learn about technologies shaping the future of marketing;
- follow the example of successful campaigns;
- find out what mobile users really want (clue: it's not a 5 per cent discount);
- make messages *do* something;
- take a hype-free look at the mobile Internet;
- discover 100 steps to mobile marketing survival.

Mobile mentors

When it comes to mobile marketing, a consensus of opinion simply does not exist. Take WAP, the 'wireless application protocol' which has made the mobile Internet a reality. Some industry experts believe the poor user experience so far means that WAP will soon be the dodo of mobile communications, usurped by more sophisticated technologies. Others, however, believe technological advances are going to bring WAP into the mainstream and lead the way towards a user-friendly and cost-effective mobile Internet.

Similarly divergent theories can be found on every other aspect of mobile marketing and technology. Text messaging, mobile spam, wireless gaming, ringtones, premium rate services, location-based shopping, mobile marketing agencies, the technological requirements, youth marketing: two views are rarely the same.

In order to reflect this diversity of opinion, each chapter includes one or more 'mobile mentor' slots, providing key players with the chance to tackle a mobile marketing issue they feel strongly about. These experts include the leading European and US figures representing industry bodies, mobile marketing agencies, service providers and technology firms. The contributions offer slightly different perspectives on each chapter's topic, and when considered together, offer an insightful cross-section of viewpoints from those on the frontline of the mobile marketing revolution.

The mobile mentors who have added their views to this book are:

Gary Andersen-Jones, Managing Director, Quartez
Marco Argenti, Managing Director, DADA Wireless (Italy)
Nikesh Arora, Board Member, T-Mobile International
Andrew Bud, CEO, mBlox
Lars Becker, CEO and Co-Founder, Flytxt
Richard England, Commercial Director, XT Marketing
John Farmer, Co-Founder, Carbon Partners
Mark Fitzgerald, Product Development Director, WAP MX
Chris Hayward, CEO, Textploitation
Richard Jesty, Senior Consultant, Arc Group
Anne de Kerckhove, Managing Director, 12Snap UK
Richard Lander, Marketing Manager, Brand2Hand
Jorge Mata, CEO, MyAlert.com (Spain)
Edward Orr, Vice President, UCP AG
Dan Pelson, Chairman and CEO, Bolt (USA)
Mark Selby, Founder, Mobile Channel Network
Mike Short, Chairman, Mobile Data Association
Jeremy Wright, Co-Founder, Enpocket
Steve Wunker, UK Chairman of the Mobile Marketing Association
   and CEO of Brainstorm

The text focus

Although other mobile technologies, such as WAP, are covered within this book, the emphasis is on text messaging. While I am happy to admit that mobile marketing has not been limited to SMS, there can be no denying that most of the major success stories have been based around this technology.

Of course, many marketers and marketing agencies have at some stage or other embraced WAP. For instance, in February 2001 Virgin Mobile rolled out its mobile shopping assistant to WAP-phone users, allowing them to do comparison shopping as well as make purchases from their wireless devices using preset preferences. Agencies such as Flytxt also incorporate WAP within their service offering along with technologies such as IVR (interactive voice response) and instant messaging.

But as Flytxt's Director of Marketing Consulting, Rick Mower, has succinctly put it, 'SMS rules because it's convenient, cheap, popular, universal and time relevant.' However, the main reason for the text message focus is because that is where the real mobile activity is. As a recent headline in a US marketing magazine rhetorically asked, 'Why ignore wireless Web applications? Because most of your customers are still ignoring them.'

Whether the 'SMS' acronym stays with us or not, it is very unlikely that the popularity of sending short text-based messages between mobile devices will diminish. When more advanced forms of mobile technology emerge, text messaging is likely to become even more popular, not less, as messages will be able to incorporate multimedia.

Furthermore, the mobile Internet, which is the sole focus of the penultimate chapter, works with rather than against text messaging. The fundamental principles of successful mobile marketing, as outlined in this book, apply to most mobile technologies. For instance, whichever technology you use, if you are contacting people via a device as personal as their mobile, it is essential to gain permission. After all, the personal nature of mobile devices, and the incredible power it offers to marketers, is unlikely to wane, even when the technology evolves.

one

The text phenomenon

The immense popularity of text messaging has, to say the very least, taken many by surprise. Conceived in the late 1980s, developed during the early 1990s and deployed almost as an afterthought, it wasn't until the close of the millennium that its true potential started to be realized.

Now, as millions of people continue to 'text' each other with ever greater enthusiasm, marketers understandably want in on the action. However, if mobile marketing is to last as a legitimate force in the long term, the nature of text messaging and the reasons underpinning its popularity need to be fully understood. With that thought in mind, this chapter zooms in for a closer look at text messaging and, with an insightful contribution from Flytxt CEO Lars Becker, looks at 'the story so far' for mobile marketing. Edward Orr, the man behind some of the largest SMS portals in existence, concludes the chapter with his own personal take on 'the messaging phenomenon'.

SMS: the quiet revolution

SMS, or the short messaging service, was the first mainstream technology to enable short text messages to be sent from one mobile device to another. Devoid of colour, graphics, audio, video, and confined to 160 characters per message, SMS hardly seemed the most radical of new media technologies. Furthermore, people wanting to send an SMS text message had to work with small, fiddly mobile keypads and tiny grey screens.

Yet for all its evident shortcomings, SMS became hugely popular and has inspired a whole generation of 'textheads', who have even conjured up their own SMS shorthand to overcome the character limit. Even among older users, SMS text messaging has proved to be a popular, less intrusive and often cost-effective alternative to voice calls.

Indeed, as will be explained in the next sub-section, the back to basics nature of SMS has been one of the main keys to its success. Even the most committed technophobe would not find it too difficult to use, even with a fiddly keypad. So while the technologists waxed lyrical about WAP and the future prospect of 3G (third generation) mobile technology, a quiet revolution was going on: a revolution very few had managed to predict.

The future prospects for SMS seem equally difficult to predict, given recent technological developments such as multimedia text messaging (MMS) and the emergence of mobile instant messenger (IM) applications. My own view is that technological developments usually happen in advance of consumer trends, and also that there will always be a way of sending short text-based messages to mobile devices. These messages may be able to incorporate additional extras (colour, graphics etc), but the fundamental factors which have made SMS a success (simplicity, low cost, convenience etc) will remain important. Text messaging will therefore evolve, but the main giant leap from voice-based mobile phones to multi-functional mobile devices has already been made with the help of SMS. Ultimately the lifespan for SMS, and the whole direction of text messaging, rests in the hands (and pockets) of the consumer.

Text benefits

As text messaging is one of the fastest growing communications technologies in human history, it is fair to assume it has a lot going for it. Although popularity is not always a guarantee of merit (just ask Britney Spears), it is unlikely that text messaging would be where it is today without having certain benefits which place it above other modes of communication. Indeed, the popularity of text messaging is itself a benefit, at least from the marketer's stand-

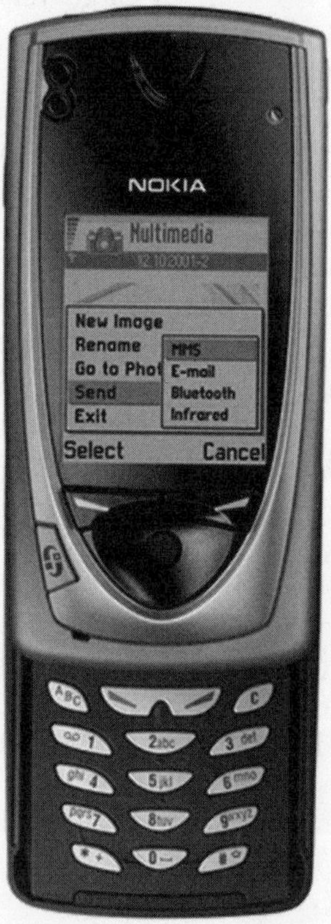

Figure 1.1 The marketing potential of the mobile medium has been opened up with the arrival of multimedia messaging

point. Furthermore, marketing messages are not the turn-off some thought they would be, and research suggests that, by 2006, 65 per cent of mobile phone subscribers will be willing to accept marketing alerts and promotions. Within the youth market, this figure has already been exceeded.

Although there are widely divergent theories as to how text messaging became so big so quickly, the following benefits have been recognized by a broad range of commentators:

● *Cost*. In those parts of the world where text messaging is starting to overtake voice calls and even e-mails, it is partly because it is a cheaper alternative. Text-message marketing campaigns also tend to be more cost-effective than other media activity (such as print or television advertising). However, the cost factor should not be over-emphasized. In fact, Finnish teenagers spend more money on mobile communications through SMS than they spend on clothing.

- *Convenience.* Although usability experts have puzzled over the success of an activity which involves using small screens and fiddly keypads, the ability to store names, numbers and keywords is adding to the convenience factor. Text messages can be sent anytime and from any place and can be composed within a couple of minutes. Furthermore, SMS conversations can be carried on in public spaces, irrespective of noise levels.
- *Immediacy.* SMS messages are also ideal for making social arrangements, with the mobile being able to store appointments and addresses as text messages. SMS messages are not only quick to compose, but they also reach the contact within a minute. Responses are often equally fast, a fact which enables mobile marketers to assess the success of a campaign in a very short timeframe.
- *Privacy.* SMS conversations remain private, even if carried out in a public location. While many feel inhibited when speaking on their mobile, for example in pubs, on public transport or with a group of friends, the same does not apply to text conversations.
- *Ubiquity.* At the time of writing there are over 700 million mobile phones worldwide with an SMS capability. One of the answers to why SMS is so popular is therefore 'because it's there to be used'. This has never been the case with WAP, at least not on the same scale.
- *Open communication.* As with e-mail, texting does not require face-to-face or voice-to-voice contact. In one study into e-mail conducted in the summer of 2000, Dr Adam Joinson of the Open University found that people are psychologically driven to disclose more when communicating via e-mails. 'They disclosed over four times as much when they communicated over the Internet as when they talked to face-to-face,' said Joinson. Likewise, texting also leads to more open communication. 'The whole thing about non-face-to-face mediums is that they're disinhibiting – people tend to reveal more about themselves

emotionally,' confirmed Dr Mark Griffiths, a psychologist from Nottingham Trent University.

Marketing benefits

In addition to these general user benefits, there are also some specific advantages for marketers:

- *Increased interaction.* 'Mobile marketing enables brands to increase their level of interaction with customers at the most appropriate time and place to deliver their marketing message,' says John Farmer, co-founder of SMS service provider Carbon Partners. 'In that sense mobile marketing delivers new opportunities for brand managers to maximize the impact of their activities.'
- *Rapid response.* Given that mobile marketing also facilitates real-time response to marketing messages, brand managers can gain rapid feedback on the effectiveness of their marketing messages across various mediums.
- *Reliability.* SMS is more reliable than most other forms of media, as there are little chances of an SMS campaign having to be rescheduled (unlike television, the Web or print, where marketers are often depending to some degree on an editorial process). Unlike other forms of new media marketing, SMS is not a particularly temperamental technology.
- *Integration.* Text messaging campaigns work well in conjunction with other media forms, especially the Web.
- *Urgency.* Given the fast and furious nature of sending and receiving text messages, SMS campaigns lend a greater sense of urgency to marketing messages.
- *Viral marketing.* As people make more connections via their mobile phone than through any other medium, the viral marketing (ie word of mouth, or 'word of text') potential is immense. Many campaigns generate more awareness from recipients contacting their friends than from the company contacting the initial 'texting list'.
- *Direct contact.* Text message exchanges enable you to get straight to the person, a task often impossible using other forms of media.

- *Segmentation.* According to mobile marketing agency 12Snap, 'targeting is possible on the basis of demographic and psychographic factors'.
- *Direct response.* The SMS- and MMS-enabled phone has a direct response capability built in. This leads to more rapid feedback.
- *Call to action.* 'Although the Internet and SMS are complimentary media, a mobile is always on, always with you, which is not the case with the Internet,' says Anne de Kerckhove from mobile marketing firm 12Snap. Ultimately, she claims, SMS provides a 'stronger call to action'.
- *Comparatively cost-effective.* Compared with other types of media marketing, text messaging can be relatively cheap.
- *Simple graphics.* While some marketers may fear that the strength of the brand can be diluted as SMS messages cannot carry their logo to consumers, there are benefits to being graphically simple. For instance, the SMS format enables users to take in and understand the marketing message, without having to cope with media 'clutter'.

Everything you ever wanted to know about text (but were afraid to ask)

Although SMS text messaging has become widely used, most people who use it know little about the way it works or how it came into being. Here are some of the key SMS facts:

- SMS was created as part of the GSM (Global System for Mobile communication) standard as a way of sending call set-up information to mobiles from an SMS centre.
- In 1992 the first SMS message was sent from a computer to a mobile phone via the UK's Vodafone network.
- The early developments were concluded in 1994 when two-way text messaging, as we now understand it, was introduced.
- SMS was never intended for mass communication.
- SMS uses the spare capacity of mobile networks.
- SMS can only carry 160 bytes of information at a time. One byte equates to one character.

- In 1998/9 internetworking, then full network connection, was established between rival UK networks.
- SMS is referred to as a 'store and forward' technology. What this means is that once a text message has been sent it will be stored (at the SMS centre) until the recipient's phone is switched on. If the phone is already switched on, the message will arrive straight away.
- All GSM phone users can potentially send and receive SMS.
- Research firm Durlacher estimates that 90 per cent of all SMS messages are person-to-person communication.
- According to Gartner Group, by 2005, over 900 million mobile phones will be in use, a majority of them in Europe and Asia. Some countries, such as Japan and Paraguay, even have more mobile phones than landline telephones, a trend expected to spread. Europe and Asia now account for over 60 per cent of cellular phones installed in the world, followed by North America and Latin America.

Mobile mentor: Lars Becker, CEO and Co-Founder of Flytxt

The story so far: the evolution of mobile marketing

We are only at the beginning of the evolution of mobile marketing. But there is already a story about its origins.

Everyone in the industry will have their own story about the beginning, but I believe that the first recognizable mobile marketing campaign ran in the hot and steamy nights and nightclubs of Ibiza in the summer of 2000. Sponsored by a UK music Web site, clubbers could get the latest goss on the clubbing scene and the most hedonistic hang-out places of the night.

The campaign was a simple alert campaign without any interactive elements, and did not request subscribers to respond to any messages. Furthermore, the sign-up was only through a Web site.

The breakthrough came later that year when Emap announced the award-winning *Smash Hits* Poptext Club, an interactive loyalty programme marketing the teen magazine. Readers could sign-up by simply sending a text message printed in the magazine and would receive new alerts, could participate in interactive games and competitions, and could also text their questions to the magazine, which would get answered in a personalized and automated way.

At the beginning of 2001 Colin Lloyd, president of the Direct Marketing

Association (DMA), predicted that as one of the trends for 2001, text messaging would take off as a marketing tool: and he was right.

In the first quarter of 2001 Channel 5 ran the first television-based mobile marketing campaign, where the audience could participate in a competition by sending in a text message. At the same time text messaging became all the rage, and the popularity of SMS rose to unprecedented levels, reaching the 1 billion messages sent per month mark. In the summer BBC1 broadcast *The Joy of Text*, a whole Saturday afternoon and evening programme entirely dedicated towards stories around SMS, including many interactive elements.

However, the outstanding campaign of 2001 was Cadbury's 'Txt'n'Win'. It was an instant win sales promotion printed on 65 million chocolate bars. With over 4 million participants, it is still the biggest and most successful mobile marketing campaign to date. Pepsi ran another, but smaller, SMS promotion at the same time.

Through these and many other promotions from major brand owners, text messaging established itself as an innovative marketing tool over the course of 2001. Initially most campaigns focused on a teen audience, while the 20–30 age bracket is now the strongest growing texting sector, and heavily targeted with text campaigns.

Anecdotally, in late 2001 Eurosport ran the first pan-European text messaging campaign promoting Warner Brothers' blockbuster *Ocean's 11* across Spain, Italy, Germany, Netherlands and the UK.

Today text messaging is used heavily by media companies to inject interactivity into their programming, used increasingly to market entertainment products like movies and music releases, and has established itself as a viable sales promotion mechanic. Other industry sectors are following suit. Consumers appear to have accepted interaction with brands through a text-only medium, limited to 160 characters.

What's next? Mobile marketing has a colourful future, in the true sense of the word. Innovation will make the interactive experience more and more appealing for consumers, also in a visual sense. But one of the key strengths of the medium is more conceptual, and independent of these innovations. Even simple text messaging enables marketers to have a more sustained impact with their marketing messages. Marketers can extend a 'broadcast' message into a dialogue with the consumer, to either let them experience some of the brand attitudes, or build an ongoing relationship with their audience.

We are truly only at the beginning.

Flytxt is a technology start-up and founding member of the Mobile Marketing Association. The firm acts as an outsourcing partner for opt-in wireless marketing services and launches wireless marketing campaigns through its campaign design, testing, reporting, ad-serving and list-management tools. Flytxt is able to handle over 10 million messages per day.

Figure 1.2 Timeout was one of the brands involved in the biggest text message campaign ever

Balearic beginnings

As Lars Becker notes, 2000 was the year mobile marketing started to take off, as SMS usage swelled across Europe. Because text messaging was still largely viewed as a youth phenomenon at this time, it was those brands attracting the youth market that were first to jump on board.

Indeed, the real testbed for SMS marketing in 2000 was the clubber's mecca, Ibiza. A variety of clubs started to offer SMS services, and some even teamed up with UK operator Orange to offer text alerts relating to the island's nightlife. Music Web site WorldPop.com ran one of the most successful and certainly more popular services. 'Ibiza was flooded with print product, so it was time to get people excited in a new way,' explains WorldPop.com's editorial director, Ben Turner. Hooking up with the Mobile Channel Network, WorldPop.com offered a Mobile Ibiza service feeding off the WorldPop Ibiza Web site, which carried club news, gossip and charts via the Internet for the entire summer.

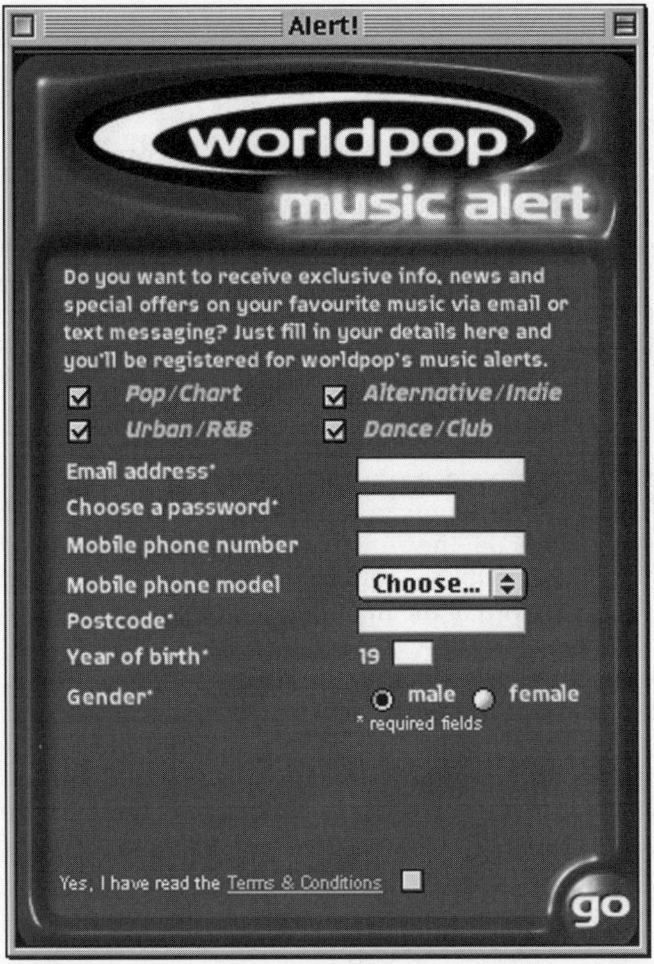

Figure 1.3 Worldpop.com's fone zone capitalizes on the brand's pioneering success in Ibiza

To make sure the service was more than just a gimmick, WorldPop and Mobile Channel Network set up a newsroom and production facilities on the island, supported by production crews across Europe. In order to give the service recognition among clubbers, it was fronted by 'superstar DJ' Pete Tong. 'This project is at the cutting edge of modern technology, much like dance music, which is why I want to be involved,' the DJ said at the time, adding a plea for holidaymakers to 'take your phone to Ibiza'. He also expressed his excitement at being 'part of a project which uses the mobile phone to its full potential'.

To register for the service, clubbers had to sign up on the WorldPop.com site with their mobile phone number and the dates they were due to be on the island. As mobile marketers have since discovered, a strong incentive is required for people to subscribe to an SMS service. When clubbers registered they were given exclusive free gifts, the most popular of which proved to be ringtones of the top ten Ibiza dance anthems. In addition, the service offered details of discounted tickets, drinks and secret parties which clubbers could not find out about from any other source.

Although the service was made available via WAP, the text message service proved more successful and remained the main focus. This was therefore an early indication that, while every one was focusing on the 'great WAP hope', SMS was the real story. Over 30,000 clubbers subscribed to the service, proving that (in Ben Turner's words) 'the mobile is integral to the clubbing experience'.

The Ibiza club scene has remained at the heart of the mobile marketing revolution, with new services launched each year designed to target the most 'hardcore' SMS devotees. Any marketer looking to attract more mainstream markets could still gain from keeping an eye on Ibiza in order to spot any potential future trends. As Jupiter MMXI analyst Noah Yasskin has observed, 'today's teen behaviour will be mainstream tomorrow'.

SMS pioneers

Although SMS marketing has only really been a force since 2000, many companies and organizations have used it to great effect. Here are some of the major brands to have stepped into the text arena:

- *Pepsi and Coca-Cola.* The fizzy drink giants have started the move away from television advertising towards more targeted SMS campaigns.
- *New Labour.* The Labour Party has sent its members SMS alerts.

- *Carlsberg.* Free beer was the incentive in one of Carlsberg's SMS campaigns.
- *Cadbury.* The confectionery giant promoted an SMS-based competition on 65 million of its chocolate bars.
- *Men's Health.* The hugely popular men's magazine has launched a text message diet service.
- *McDonald's.* The burger chain ran a year-long text messaging campaign in a joint venture with mobile marketing agency 12Snap. It still uses SMS as part of its activity.
- *Heineken.* Heineken has used SMS to send out sports scores for events that it sponsors. It also used SMS in China to market its SuperClub dance parties, where winners of a drawing were informed via SMS.
- *Cosmopolitan.* *Cosmopolitan* offers its readers SMS alerts on how to improve their sex lives.

SME SMS

However, it is not just large brands who have been leading the way by incorporating SMS into their marketing activity. Here are examples of SMEs using SMS creatively:

- *The Brew Crew.* This Dublin-based drinks company ran a successful 'Win a Keg of Beer' SMS competition.
- *Chapple Davis.* This PR company with music industry clients offers an alert service regarding those artists subscribers want to hear about.
- *Rent-a-flat.* Oxford-based letting agents and property managers Rent-a-flat notify house hunters the moment a new property meeting their requirements becomes available.
- *Greenstuff.* This organic food company uses an SMS tracking system, to enable customers to get information about their meat. 'They can track a joint of beef from the supermarket shelf right back to the farm,' says Greenstuff's Managing Director Conor Brenan.

A limited canvas

One of the reasons some marketers are still a little reluctant to leap out of their swizzle chairs and get all excited about SMS is because, let's be frank, it is visually the 'plain Jane' of communications media. It currently allows little opportunity for aesthetic creativity other than quirky little text-based images. This is, after all, a medium relying on a monochrome, text-only, tiny mobile display to communicate messages. Furthermore, marketers typically only have 160 characters with which to express their message.

However, what are seen as limitations could just as easily be viewed as benefits. The fact that SMS messages are so limited in format means that marketing promotions look similar to texts sent from a mobile user's friend. Consequently, the divide between commercial and personal messages is narrowed, and so, providing the messages are of value and are permission-based, they are usually well received.

Furthermore, it enables marketers of all sizes and budgets to compete on the same terms. Although large brands may have more technological resources at their disposal, it is just as easy for a small company to create an attractive text message. With SMS, what you say has become just as important as how you say it.

Ultimately though, this does not lessen the challenges for marketers, but raises them. They have to ensure that every message they deliver is directly relevant to each user, and that it arrives in an appropriate context. Once this can be achieved, the opportunities are boundless.

Types of campaign

As mobile marketing is the youngest and most innovative form of marketing, every successful campaign adds something fresh to the mix. As a result, it is difficult to narrow the field down into types. However, it is possible to identify the following broad trends:

- *Competitions.* Promotional 'text to win' competitions are proving increasingly popular among marketers. Often, these are promoted via non-mobile media (television, posters, products, in-store etc) and require participants to text their entry to a designated number.
- *Free downloads.* Campaigns are often centred around the promise of free downloads, typically for ringtones and logos. Once mobile users have requested the download, they may then be asked if they want to receive ongoing promotional material. This is a method adhered to by many Internet portals.
- *Special offers.* Ongoing promotional material is often in the form of carefully targeted special offers. Providing the offer is strong enough, this tactic can also be used to initiate a campaign.
- *Loyalty clubs.* Perk-based loyalty clubs are another popular means of building brand–customer relations via text messaging.
- *Shopping channels.* Mobile shopping channels such as the UK-based ZagMe enable retailers to target consumers at relevant locations.
- *News.* Companies providing newsworthy promotional information (such as a new product launch), or more objective news with the intention of building relations, find SMS the perfect platform.
- *Internet campaigns.* Mobile Internet campaigns, based around WAP (Wireless Application Protocol) and other technologies, have so far had mixed success.
- *Alerts.* One of the most prevalent commercial uses of SMS to emerge has been the area of user-requested updates and alerts, delivered through either push or pull methods. Customers can either subscribe to a service that will provide regular alerts on a chosen subject (match results, clubbing news etc) or request information by sending a key word via SMS.
- *Gaming.* In some countries branded gaming has emerged, its novelty and mobility proving more than enough compensation for the low-bandwidth styles.

Beyond the youth market

For the majority of young people in Europe, text messaging is now the preferred way to communicate. According to a Childwise

Monitor report, 90 per cent of teenagers use text messaging instead of speaking on their mobiles. The days when texting was the sole preserve of the youth market are now over. AT Kearney and Cambridge University Business School of Research have found that SMS usage among older age groups is now growing faster than in teen audiences. By 2001, parents were discovering that SMS is a good way to stay in touch with their children. This was reflected in campaigns such as the Harry Potter SMS campaign, which attempted to turn SMS messaging into a family experience, with both parents and teenagers invited to text-in to win free tickets.

There has also been an increase in older users. A September 2001 survey conducted by Mori on behalf of the Internet bank Egg discovered that text messaging is increasingly popular among over-55s. The survey found that there were over one million active 'silver texters' in the UK. This indicated that mobile marketers who, up until that time, had focused their sights primarily on the media-saturated 15–34 age group, could find equally lucrative markets higher up the age scale. The survey also highlighted that the over-55s are using an increasing variety of technologies. 'The chances are that not only will you have access to at least some interactive technologies, but your mother or even your grandmother will too,' said Mark Nancarrow, the Chief Operating Officer of Egg, when the survey findings were first published. 'And even more staggeringly, they will probably be using them for more than simply looking up the weather forecast.'

Mobile mentor: Edward Orr, Vice President of UCP AG

An overview of SMS: the messaging phenomenon

Even my ultra-conservative old boss has heard of SMS now. He still claims it is too complicated for him to use but he is fully aware of its existence, popularity and importance in the communication mix. However, SMS does face scepticism from two extremes. One extreme is from the technological Luddities who confuse share prices with social relevance and think that the Internet has been a failure, and on the other are the technological optimists who are confident that SMS will imminently be superseded by much more advanced technologies. As ever, the reality is somewhere between the two extremes.

Like e-mail, SMS has undeniably been a huge success in terms of person-to-person communication. However, there are still issues to be resolved in fully harnessing it for other commercial purposes such as marketing and value-added SMS products and services, and all the time that those issues are being worked out, so are more advanced technologies such as 3G being worked on. However, not only will it take quite a long time (maybe as much as five years) for the new mobile technologies to reach the same level of mass market penetration as SMS, it is actually directly through the evolution of messaging from SMS to enhanced and multi-media messaging (EMS and MMS) that the new mobile technologies are most likely gain widespread acceptance.

Initially SMS wasn't aggressively promoted. It was a grassroots revolution led by the youth market. The messaging generation initially adopted this technology because they could appropriate it for themselves: it was theirs, not their parents' or their teachers' or the operators' (the operators were actually busy trying to dictate the adoption of WAP).

However, after the explosive growth of the initial messaging revolution, SMS has carried on growing to achieve ever-wider adoption because it has certain genuine advantages. Firstly, penetration rates of mobile phones are rapidly approaching 80 per cent of the population (much higher than Internet penetration) and almost all those phones are GSM phones that support SMS, so there is almost ubiquitous availability. Secondly it is relatively cheap. It is also visual (ie text or image) and that suits certain types of communication better than voice. It is personal: it goes straight to a person's unique handset. Most of all, it is mobile: it can be received any time, anywhere.

Given the current economic environment, especially for new media, the marketing industry is being slow to recognize and resistant to adopting SMS as a fundamental part of the communication mix of today's society, in the same way that operators were slow to recognize the real economic value of person-to-person SMS and that the music industry has been sticking its head in the sand on ringtones (the most successful SMS 'product' so far), despite the fact that people often pay more for a ringtone than a CD single. Forget all the acronyms (SMS, MMS, GPRS, UMTS etc etc), non-voice mobile communication is already here. It is huge and it is here to stay and it is in everyone's interests to accept that and start working with it now in its current mass market form, SMS.

Edward Orr is a Vice President of UCP AG, a specialist in mobile Internet technologies that has over 5 million registered users of its consumer SMS portals uboot.com and sms.at.

Text versus Web

In a Probe Research 2001 report, entitled 'Wireless advertising: start-up profiles and market projections', the benefits of Internet advertising were compared with marketing via text messages. The author of the report (Ann Lynch, Probe's co-director of wireless Internet services) found that, with recall rates of 58 per cent and click-through rates of 10 per cent (compared with 0.5 per cent for the fixed Internet), text has a greater potential than its online counterpart.

The proactive, opt-in nature of text message campaigns was seen to be much more effective than Web banners and other forms of Internet advertising. Indeed, the wireless medium as a whole has been seen to lend itself to more targeted and personal forms of advertising. 'It's a service that I choose and I control,' Lynch said, in an interview with MforMobile.com. 'There is no escape from other forms of advertising but here the user controls the type and frequency of the message and that is what sells users (like me) on it.'

The Probe report concluded with a warning for the wireless portals, starting that the wireless ad developers (such as Flytxt and 12Snap) could eventually push them out of the picture. Indeed, some have argued that, 12 months on from when the report was published, this was already starting to happen, as the mobile marketing firms bypassed the portals to work directly with operators.

Last word

Although it takes courage to embrace any new medium, the sheer popularity of text messaging alone means that businesses can no longer afford to wait passively on the sidelines. When global brands such as Coca-Cola start to move away from television advertising in order to focus on SMS, it is time to sit up and take notice. Furthermore, the fact that smaller companies have had success with text message campaigns means that mobile marketing has real opportunities for every business, regardless of size or budget. Moreover, the majority of those companies that have run text messaging campaigns are sticking with the medium in future. The only question is, how long will it be before everyone else starts to get the message?

two

The mobile mindset

As this book will reiterate, the key to putting together a successful campaign has little to do with technology and a lot to do with understanding the personal nature of the mobile medium. Of course, the technology is important. Essential, in fact. But success is determined not by whether or not you can send out messages, but by the context within which they are delivered. Mobile marketing involves a radical rethink regarding how we interact with customers and how we build brands. This chapter seeks to explain the unique challenges and opportunities this medium presents, and the way they can be managed successfully.

Permission marketing

The term 'permission marketing' refers to any marketing activity that depends on the permission of consumers. Permission, or opt-in, marketing first became a big issue when e-mail inboxes became inundated with junk or 'spam' messages. If anything, though, the need for permission is even greater when it comes to mobile marketing.

The mobile phone is possibly the most personal communications technology ever to have existed. Despite this, some companies have obtained thousands of mobile numbers and sent unsolicited text messages, otherwise known as 'mobile spam', to unsuspecting users. The danger is that such activity could seriously jeopardize the whole future of mobile marketing, and so various national and international organizations such as the Mobile Marketing Association (MMA) have started to clamp down on the problem.

As I will discuss in Chapter 5, 'Responsible marketing', the main reason not to get involved in the practice – aside from ethical reasons – is that it doesn't work. A permission-based approach is essential because it enables you to know who your audience is, and it is only by gaining this audience knowledge that the message can have the desired effect. As Mark Guthrie, the UK Managing Director of mobile marketing specialist AirMedia, remarked in an *M-commerce World* article (www.m-commerceworld.com), 'by definition spam is a message you are not interested in, so the likelihood of converting these messages to revenue is lower than if you had taken the time to ask personal details in the first place'.

Think narrow

Along with the Internet and (to a lesser extent) digital television, mobile technology has led to a fundamental shift in the way marketers can get their messages out. A decade or so ago, when media meant little more than print, radio and television, the options available to marketers were limited. Although there were local newspapers, radio stations and television programmes, targeting audiences via media campaigns was still a risky business. As broadcast media has always been one-way (marketer to consumer, never the other way around), and as they often reached a cross-section of the population, evaluating the success of a campaign inevitably involved an element of guesswork.

However, the arrival of new media forms, coupled with the evolution of old ones, has led to an age of micro-media and, in turn, to micro-marketing. Companies no longer need to broadcast their messages; they can (in theory, at least) narrowcast them to smaller, more targeted audiences. In addition, advances in mobile technology mean that marketers can interact with their customers in a way that was impossible before. Every message sent out can be monitored, and every response can be accounted for, providing there is a call to action.

Of course, mobile media such as SMS have not and will not replace other types of media, and marketers should not pretend to inhabit a brave new world where mobile is all that matters. Indeed, some of the most successful campaigns have integrated mobile technology with the use of commercial mass media. However, marketers who choose to ignore mobile technology are in effect ignoring one of the most powerful ways of reaching and actively engaging their target customers.

Mobile branding

For most people, the word 'brand' is often associated with a visual signifier: the Nike swoosh, the golden 'M' of McDonald's, the red and white of the Virgin logo. However, for mobile marketers, particularly those using SMS, the visual aspect of branding must take a back seat. That is not to say that branding is not important for SMS marketers. It is, if anything, more important. A brand is a company's overall image, and visual image is only a small, superficial part of this. The image is created by 'usefulness' (a loose but unavoidable term) and the company's perceived values. It is often seen as an association: for instance, Volvo's branding consolidates the notion of 'safety'.

SMS, along with e-mail, offers a new form of branding based on interactivity. Since text messaging (like other wireless technology) is a user-initiated medium, marketers must not only become excellent conveyors of their message, but also exceptional listeners.

The old view of branding was essentially as a one-way activity. Brand managers would lock themselves away, brainstorm, and then deliver their brand message to an unsuspecting public. In the wireless age, this approach is no longer sustainable. As Ray Bango, CEO of Bango.net has commented, 'a mobile phone is a life support system, it is not a mind control device'. Branding via mobile is therefore about engaging in conversation. Brand managers who continue to soliloquize into the void and hope for the best are unlikely to find an eager audience.

However, it is important to remember that SMS branding is a two-way process. As M-Corp's Jeremy Hamilton has advised, 'the starting point is to focus on the target customers, particularly their needs and expectations'. If marketers ignore the requirements of their customers by sending spam of blatant sales messages, there can be a negative impact. As David Weinberger, co-author of *The*

Cluetrain Manifesto, has pointed out, 'markets are getting more connected and more powerfully vocal every day'. Although Weinberger was writing about the Internet, text messaging has also made connections within markets stronger. If a brand strategy is misguided, a reverse viral effect can occur, whereby 'word of text' works against the marketing campaign.

Building an infobrand

In order to keep customers on side, mobile marketers need to make sure they are offering genuinely useful information. The dilemma lies in balancing this information with the message you want to get across. Internet marketers have for years been trying to find the perfect balance or ratio between promotion and information. In mobile marketing, especially SMS, this balance may seem even more difficult to achieve. After all, how much promotion and how much information do you fit into a message limited to 160 characters? Do you allocate 80 to each? Of course you don't.

For companies that really take their CRM activity seriously, the solution is to convert the information into the brand message itself. In other words, for wireless marketing activity to succeed, the consumer should not even be able to make a distinction between useful information and the information a brand wants to get across. 'The mobile medium is distinctly different and as such the marketing message should reflect this,' says Carbon Partners' co-founder, John Farmer. 'Mobile marketing is about relevant information delivered at an appropriate time for the recipient.' This is indeed true, but 'relevancy' must apply equally to both the recipient and the sender.

The trick is to make sure the product or service you are offering is part of the information package. This is, of course, easier for some brands than others. For instance, when *Men's Health* magazine launched its SMS diet service, it worked because the messages provided relevant information, but at the same time strengthened the brand. The text messages were a natural extension of the magazine's content.

However, even if you don't have an information-based product, it is still possible to build an infobrand. A retailer of health products

could offer a similar service, incorporating its own good
the advice. Similarly, a cosmetics firm could provide an SMS
service offering special promotions relating to certain tips. And
those within the service industry have a particular advantage here,
especially if it is their business to give advice. Lawyers, accountants,
insurers – even marketing consultants – can all use SMS to build
and sustain relations with their key clients. In fact, it is hard to
imagine a brand which couldn't be successfully, erm, infobranded.

Even Pampers, the nappy company, managed to successfully
infobrand itself by offering a Mother and Baby help line. The perfect
ration between promotion and information provision is therefore no
longer 50:50, but 100:100.

Adding real value

The mobile phone has been referred to as a 'see-saw' marketing tool.
In other words, it doesn't work if all the activity – or weight – comes
from the side of the marketer. For text messaging, and indeed the
mobile Internet, to truly work in your favour it therefore also needs
to work in favour of the consumer. As Steven Griffin, Marketing
Manager of mobile services at IDT Global in the UK, observes,
'essentially mobile new media is just another form of communication with the consumer, and as the marketers endeavour to pene-
trate ever more deeply into people's lives, they must realize that in
order to "own" the consumer they need to work for the consumer
by continually adding value to their daily lives'.

Real value is not a '5 per cent off while stocks last' coupon; it is
something customers feel they already want. So what, then, do
mobile users really, really want? Here is just a selection of things
which you may, or may not, be able to offer. Either way, there is no
denying their strong attraction:

- *Money.* Okay, so it's hardly original, but cash incentives – such
  as competition prizes – are unlikely to ever go out of fashion.
- *Free airtime.* You are probably unable to offer it, but free airtime
  – as the success of Hong Kong's Spotcast service testifies – is the
  ultimate gift for any mobile user.
- *Free anything.* Actually, free anything is always welcome. Of
  course, if the product offered for free is directly relevant to your

business then it will make more sense, both for you and the subscriber. Carlsberg's 'free beer' SMS campaign proved particularly successful.

- *Ringtones.* Love them or hate them, downloadable ringtones are – along with SMS itself – the major m-commerce success story. They also provide a very strong incentive for mobile users to subscribe to an SMS service, especially if they are relevant. For instance, WorldPop's Ibiza Clubbing News service ringtones of the 'top ten Ibiza anthems' were made available on registration.
- *Logos.* As with ringtones, logos have been a massive hit, especially with the youth market. Obviously, from marketers' points of view, it is ideal if the logos are of their brand or company. However, you must again think from the user's perspective. If you are Manchester United this is clearly a good strategy; if you are a toilet seat manufacturer it clearly isn't.
- *Games.* The arrival of 'retro' games such as Space Invaders has helped to move the mobile gaming market into the mainstream. Free downloadable branded games – no matter how simple – have helped many marketers to get their message across. For instance, Nestlé launched KitKat-sponsored games on mobiles.
- *Location services.* Location-based services, such as Brainstorms UK shopping service, provide consumers with tangible value.
- *Exclusive news.* Many firms offering 'exclusive news' services as part of a marketing campaign are, in fact, offering blatant sales material. However, text messaging is the perfect medium for providing genuinely informative 'news bites'. The more tailored the news can be, the more likely it will be useful to the target users.
- *Practical information.* Information people can use and act on – such as the *Men's Health* SMS diet service – is even more likely to be of value.
- *Communication services.* Any service which can help people communicate with their peers – such as the highly popular location-based 'flirt services' – is likely to be effective, as it acknowledges the primary function of a mobile device.

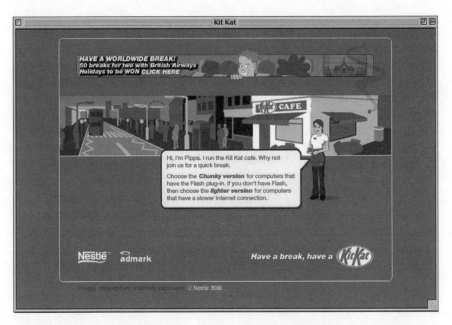

Figure 2.1   KitKat reached out to mobile gamers

Mobile mentor: Jorge Mata, CEO, MyAlert.com, Spain

When and where: the two factors for mobile marketing success

The way I see mobile marketing is as an event-driven personalized experience, enriched by 'where' (location) and 'when' (time) variables. Of course, such personalization has not been possible via the fixed Internet. Let me illustrate it with an example.

Mike gets out of work and starts walking towards the car park. On his way there he receives an alert on his mobile phone reminding him of his son's birthday tomorrow. He then decides to go to the nearest shopping centre before going home. Once in the shopping mall, Mike receives an alert from a nearby retailer offering a discount of 20 per cent on a suitable present for his kid's birthday. He decides to enter the store and show the message to the salesmen there.

What we see in the example is mobile marketing at its best: it is personalized, and uses location and time to enrich the experience. However, the personalization is not linked to a browsing concept, as it is on the PC Internet. This browsing concept, so obvious with regard to the PC Internet, becomes different in the mobile world. This is because mobile phones are used on the go. Mobile devices have become the remote controls of our day-to day living. They can be tuned to respond to personal profiles, since they have the technology required (SMS) to grab our attention when something of interest happens. And it is the user who defines what is interesting, and when. Personalizing 'what' content to 'which' user is very important. If I am on the street walking to the nearest taxi station, I might not be in the best position to navigate through my phone and look for the best bike deal. But if I am alerted by the nearest shop about a great offer for my son's birthday, the guys at the shop are likely to have made my day.

In the example given, location plays an important role. The store knows it has to make an offer to Mike once he is located 200 metres away from the store. Consequently, Mike is enticed to enter the store. All retailers know that when this happens there is already a 70 per cent probability of a sale. In any case, the personalization profile increases the likelihood of a sale thanks to the location variable. The profile of the user is enriched with the information of where he/she is right now. In particular, location-based services are very promising in connection with the Yellow Pages service. This provides a multi-channel content directory application displaying information about restaurants, gas stations, cinemas and so on, based on an end user's location.

The time variable in the profile plays a very important role. In the example above, the alert is only fired once Mike is out of the office and on the way to the car park. After all, an alert during office hours would have the same impact as an e-mail alert. Timing is therefore as important as location.

When timing and location can be perfectly matched, all types of scenario can become possible. For instance, auctions can be run just 20 minutes before playing a movie to sell off remaining seats, and the user can pick up the ticket right at the entrance of the theatre. Bets can be placed in real time as a soccer match is happening, differentiating between people watching on television and those at the stadium.

However, we need to understand that appropriate timing can cause a 'bottleneck' in mobile marketing, particularly regarding real-time events. For instance, if an alert is sent every time a team scores a goal in a soccer match, the value of this service rests on how 'real' real time can be. Experience shows that users of such a service experience a one minute delay from the time the team scores to the time they receive the alert on the mobile phone. Now, think of 100,000 users signing up for a Real Madrid–Manchester United game: that means 100,000 messages need to be received in less than a minute, or 1.700 personalized and sponsored messages per second – a bandwidth that most Telcos cannot provide, and that most software platforms cannot provide.

Timing in mobile SMS applications is extremely linked to the scalability of the service. This is exacerbated in new technologies like GPRS and UMTS where we will see that timing is intrinsically linked to geographical bandwidth. We might want to sponsor a real-time auction at the entrance of a soccer stadium, but do we have enough bandwidth covering the stadium to maintain 100,000 simultaneous users?

Jorge Mata is founder and CEO of MyAlert.com. Prior to starting MyAlert, he was Vice President of Services for Broadvision Europe. He was previously the New Channels VP at Banco Santander, where he designed Internet banking solutions and the first European GSM banking solution. Jorge holds an MS in Physics from Universidad Autonoma (Madrid), and an MBA from New York University (NYC).

Pull and push

In basic terms, mobile marketing divides into two categories: pull and push. As the term implies, pull marketing involves the consumer pulling information towards him or herself. In push marketing, it is down to the marketer to send or push messages out to the consumer.

The terms 'pull' and 'push' are also applied to other forms of promotional activity. For instance, direct mail generally falls into the pull bracket, while setting up a promotional Web site, which users can then choose to visit or not, is considered a pull activity (Web banners, on the other hand, fall largely into the push category).

In mobile marketing, and specifically text message marketing, pull and push differentiates between a subscription-based campaign where recipients are sent mass messages over an ongoing period (push), and information or services sent instantly as the result of a specific, often personalized request (pull). Typically, in a push-based campaign each message promotes a product, while in the pull-based model the message is the product, or at least enables the relevant transaction to occur. There are advantages of both types and, as discussed below, significant problems that need to be overcome if your marketing activity, whether push or pull, is to succeed.

Push marketing problems

Push marketing has traditionally been the most widely adopted model for text message marketers. A standard push campaign involves the consumers signing up to receive offers and updates from a company. The consumers will then be sent these offers/updates at regular intervals until they become bored and decide to opt out.

The most obvious advantage of this model is that it usually requires little effort on the part of the consumer to initiate the campaign, and the marketer can then send out mass messages to opt-in subscribers simultaneously. However, a number of problems have also been associated with push marketing, such as:

● *Switching media.* Although push campaigns require minimal effort for consumers to continue receiving alerts (once they have opted in they just have to wait for the next message), extra effort is required if they want to act on these messages. In order to make a transaction they often have to visit a Web site or make a voice call. This creates inertia within a campaign, and many companies have found it difficult to keep the consumer's level of interest high enough to switch medium and format. Obviously, for campaigns that require no such media-switch this is not an issue.

● *Bad timing.* Timing needs to be extremely well considered when sending out push messages. Sometimes there may be an obvious time to send. For instance, the SMS campaign for *Top of the Pops* magazine sent its messages out during the *Top of the Pops* television show. When there is no obvious time to send, it is advisable to ask the subscribers to choose their own timeslots when they sign up. Even then, however, there is no guarantee that these times, often chosen weeks or months in advance, will remain appropriate.

● *Diminishing returns.* There is often a law of diminishing returns at work in push campaigns. The message most likely to be received is the one sent closest to the sign-up time. The further away from the point of subscription, the less interest the consumer is likely to have in the campaign.

● *Spam.* Even if a subscriber has signed up for a service, push marketers have to be careful to avoid the spam accusation. If a message arrives out of context, or a long time after the original subscription, it may be viewed as unsolicited.

It should be pointed out that all four of the above are only potential problems. Many push campaigns have managed to bypass each of them successfully. Even where the law of diminishing returns does apply, the campaign can still be worthwhile for both marketer and consumer, if only to build brand awareness.

That said, pull marketing has emerged as a valid alternative, as it takes many of these problems away. In a pull service, the marketer waits until the user sends a message, and then responds to that request. The risks of bad timing, diminishing returns and spam are therefore avoided altogether.

'One of the huge benefits you can get from pull services is that you find out what your user really wants,' states Robert Hamilton on the M-commerce world Web site (www.mcommerceworld.com). 'This information can be enormously valuable when planning new services as spontaneous requests from users are a very good guide to their tastes.'

Pull marketing problems

Although pull marketing is often heralded as the best possible way to build relations with mobile users, it too has its drawbacks. Here are a few of the main areas:

● *Format limitations*. The idea behind most pull campaigns is that the mobile users get instant access to the information or service they want. The problem for mobile marketers is that they have to provide this information within the inherent limitations of the text message. While advancements in WAP, GPRS, MMS and 3G may ultimately make this a non-issue, in the meantime marketers adopting pull-based models need to be able to find a way of providing real value in 160 characters.

● *Consumer cost*. Although premium rates enable marketers to generate extra revenue, often shared with the mobile operators, they do act as a consumer deterrent. Furthermore, unlike push marketing models, in which consumers only have to send out, in pull marketing consumers have to pay every time they want to receive information.

- *Lack of information.* Control is given over to the consumer in a pull campaign, in that marketers are unable to say when a message should be sent out. In order to maximize their chances of generating repeat interest, marketers need to encourage users to store their number within the mobile device's memory.
- *Marketing cost.* Owing to the extra requirements, in terms of personalization and so on, the marketing cost is higher than in push campaigns.

Viral marketing

The term 'viral marketing' was first coined by venture capitalist Steve Jurveston in 1997, to describe the Internet's ability to fuel interest in a product or service. Jurveston was trying to explain the phenomenal rise of the free Web-based e-mail service that he had initially helped finance the previous year.

Hotmail remains the archetypal viral marketing example. Within a year of its launch, the service had accumulated 10 million registered users. This feat is even more remarkable when you consider that this was achieved with a marketing budget of only US$50,000 (for Silicon Valley in the late 1990s, this was small change). Needless to say, this was before Microsoft bought the company.

According to Jurveston, Hotmail's rapid success was a direct result of a decision to include a short band of text at the bottom of every e-mail sent by a Hotmail user. The band of text read: 'Get your free Web based e-mail at Hotmail'. The line also incorporated a hyperlink that sent the recipient to Hotmail's home page. This meant that the very act of sending a Hotmail message constituted an endorsement of the service. As a result, a 'viral' effect occurred, whereby Hotmail customers spread the word simply by using the service itself. The recipients of a Hotmail message learnt not only that the service is effective, but also that their friend or colleague was a user.

The principle behind viral marketing is simple. If customers are telling each other about a product or service, the message is going to be more effective than the company itself directly communicating with potential customers. As viral marketing guru Seth Godin writes in his e-book, *Unleashing the Idea Virus* (itself a viral phenomenon), 'with word of mouse you can tell 100 friends, or a thousand friends. Because the numbers are larger and faster than they are offline, the virus grows instead of slows.'

However, if 'word of mouse' is effective, 'word of text' can be even more powerful. As mobiles are habitually used for social communication, the opportunities for enhancing the effectiveness of marketing messages via identifiable communities of interest are very strong indeed. The viral potential of mobile marketing has been recognized since 2000, when wireless services company Quios' Euro 2000 messaging service proved a massive 'word of text' success. 70 per cent of users surveyed by Quios after the service finished said that they had recommended it to friends.

The aim for any mobile marketer is to maximize the viral impact of any service or campaign:

- *Create a consumer-to-consumer environment.* According to Seth Godin, 'it's imperative to stop marketing at people. The idea is to create an environment where consumers will market to each other.'
- *Have confidence in your service.* 'One of the beautiful things about viral marketing or word of mouth or buzz in general is that all these mechanisms only work when you're talking about a good product,' says Emanuel Rosen, author of *The Anatomy of Buzz*. Therefore unless you can be absolutely sure that your SMS service is good enough for users to spread the word, you may need to rethink.
- *Surprise your subscribers.* In the very early days of mobile marketing, messages contained a degree of surprise through the lack of clutter. As consumers grow accustomed to receiving commercial messages and as 'text fatigue' starts to set in, marketers can no longer rely on an automatic wow factor.
- *Make a strong offer.* For viral marketing to work, the original offer needs to be a strong one.
- *Encourage interactivity.* Irish SMS service provider Puca created a system for users to chat, create online profiles and search for compatible dates, all via their mobile phones. The Puca Community platform, on which the product is based, was designed to enable companies to enhance a Web-only presence with interactive community features using WAP or SMS. Such platforms provide perfect viral marketing opportunities because, as with the case of Hotmail, the service itself centres around person-to-person communication.

New York Celebrity Sightings: learn from a viral phenomenon

Although the lack of a uniform mobile standard has prevented the SMS revolution from taking a firm grip of the United States, there is no shortage of US companies willing to make creative use of text messaging. Not least among these is Upoc, a New York based wireless startup.

The company's main project is the now infamous New York Celebrity Sightings, a wireless messaging group that has proved a hit among starry-eyed mobile users in the Big Apple. Members who sign up for the service are able to send messages informing others every time they spot a celebrity. According to Upoc's CEO, Gordon Gould, the secret to the success of Celebrity Sightings is the fact that it is simple to use, as well as helping the users to gain recognition from their peers. 'It's very obvious and apparent to people what the rules are,' he said. 'If I see a celebrity – bang! – I send a message. That's really easy. All of a sudden I'm culturally relevant.'

Given the amount of people who evidently feel the need to know which bagel bar Johnny Depp goes to, where David Duchovny buys a kiddie car seat, or what Courtney Cox Arquette gets up to on a Sunday afternoon, Upoc are clearly onto a winner (over 10 per cent of Upoc's members subscribe to the service). Members are typically sent one message a day, although this number increases dramatically when there is an entertainment industry gathering such as an awards ceremony in town. Similar Celebrity Sightings services are also expected elsewhere, both in the United States and worldwide. Although this type of service will only ever be a niche offering, it does provide marketers with a good idea of what makes a viral campaign work. As mentioned, simplicity and cultural relevancy play a part, but there are other reasons too. These include:

- *The pass-it-on factor.* Given the unique 'pass it on' nature of the service, word spreads from members to non-members.
- *Peer-to-peer content.* With Celebrity Sightings, content is taken care of by the service users themselves. This not only means that Upoc can save on resources, but also that the content becomes even more relevant to members. After all, they are creating it.

- *Location sensitivity*. According to Cynthia Haswe, a wireless analyst at the Strategis Group, Celebrity Sightings is a prime example of what end users want from an SMS service. 'It makes sense in the end because it is location-sensitive,' she says.
- *Time sensitivity*. As well as being location-sensitive, the service is also time-sensitive. This gives each message an added relevancy.
- *Fun*. The fun element to services like Celebrity Sightings adds to the 'viral' element.

As well as mobile users, media companies have also seen the value in Upoc's service. For instance, Sony's Columbia Group has used the service to send subscribers personalized messages. 'Ultimately we're providing a bridge between entertainment companies, sponsors and wireless carriers,' says Gould.

Alongside Celebrity Sightings, Upoc also runs a Mullet Watch service, whereby any time someone spots someone sporting a haircut beloved of 1980s football stars, they can send an SMS alert. 'This is not like a corporate product,' Gould told Wired, 'but it is the kind of thing people are actively amused by'. The self-explanatory Hot Bartenders service operates in a similar fashion.

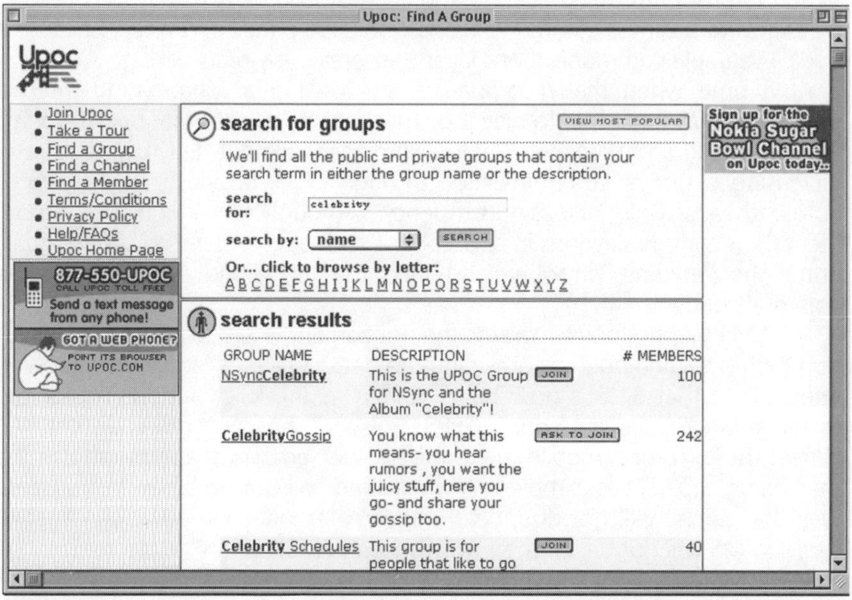

Figure 2.2 Upoc.com offers a wide variety of text message groups

Mobile mentor: Gary Andersen-Jones, Managing Director, Quartez Ltd

SMS needs to overcome a cultural mindset

The current success of SMS lies in its simplicity. Easy to use, quick to deliver and cheap to process, SMS usage has grown virally within the consumer-to-consumer space over the past three years. Teenagers have led the way, making SMS the killer mobile application for young consumers who account for a large portion of the 40 million text messages that, according to the Mobile Data Association (November 2001), are sent every day in the UK.

So if it's such a cost-effective, instant messaging medium, why aren't businesses using it more? The fact that you can make money from it through premium rate reverse billing should start an avalanche of businesses eager to sign up for SMS services.

Like fax, then e-mail before it, SMS is facing a cultural barrier in business. So far, business usage of text messaging extends to competitions on chocolate wrappers, viewer/listener comment for television and radio stations, sports results services and a wide range of daily horoscope-type messages. It's a start, but like e-mail, SMS should have a greater destiny.

SMS should be helping businesses cut traditional communications overheads, improve internal processes and increase company visibility. It needs to be critical to business communications alongside e-mail and voice, because it adds a valuable communications layer that previously didn't exist.

At a time when many companies are looking at automating internal processes, SMS has a role to play too. Through the use of Enterprise Resource Planning (ERP) and Employee Relationship Management (ERM) systems, and increasing customer communication through CRM, businesses are trying to cut overheads while increasing efficiency. Although e-mail is usually fundamental for communications in applications such as these, e-mail cannot guarantee the 'anytime, anywhere' scenario that is second nature to mobile communications.

The SMS sceptics point towards the horizon and the dawn of new generation mobile technologies as providing the death knell for SMS as we know it. The truth is that SMS is now being touted as the killer application for the forthcoming mobile networks, GPRS, 3G and the even more distant 4G. While these future mobile generations will enable graphics and video messaging capabilities, simple text messaging will not go away. In the same way that e-mail will not disappear with greater videoconferencing capabilities, so SMS will not be usurped by MMS and EMS.

So if SMS is here to stay, it makes sense for businesses to take it more seriously and start thinking about how they can use it to not only save money, but make money.

Gary Andersen-Jones is Managing Director of Quartez, an SMS solutions and gateway provider, which offers intelligent mobile and business process integration using the short messaging service (SMS). He has written for a variety of national newspapers including the Guardian, Daily Mirror *and* The Times Educational Supplement, *as well as a large number of magazines, including consumer magazines such as* Moneywise *and business titles like* PC Dealer.

Last word

The mobile medium requires us to look at the whole concept of marketing afresh. No longer can the dividing lines between 'them' (the consumers) and 'us' (the marketers) be upheld. The personal and two-way nature of mobile means that marketers need to engage in conversation with mobile users on their own terms. After all, the mobile device itself gives people more power not only to interact with companies, but also to decline or accept marketing messages. However, for those marketers willing to provide real value, this power can work in their favour. The potential for viral marketing has never been greater, as marketers are now able to pass the brand-building baton over to consumers themselves.

three

The mobile marketing menu

Mobile technology provides companies with a brave new world of marketing options. Whether you are promoting a product launch, looking for an extra revenue channel or building relations over the long term, you now have improved means of doing so. However, not every choice available on the mobile marketing menu will be suitable for every brand or business. This chapter therefore does not aim to tell you what method you should choose. What it does do is to provide you with further information in order for you to make up your own mind.

Premium services

Premium services are accounting for a rapidly growing proportion of SMS services, particularly in Europe. Indeed, SMS content-rich services are expected to be worth £2.4 billion in the EC by 2006. Already premium services are proving popular, constituting approximately 10 per cent of the entire text messaging market. If we take the model of mobile operator Orange as an example, it reveals that mobile users are willing to pay three times more for premium services than they are for person-to-person communication. (As well as operating its own network services, Orange works with various content providers on its own branded campaigns.) Premium services such as the Bridget Jones Text Diary have proved just how attractive they can be to subscribers. However, although prices for premium SMS services vary significantly, premium services depend on a high demand.

Helen Fielding, sending text messages as Bridget, was always going to have a hit on her hands. Other marketers wanting to offer premium rate services need to make sure their proposition is equally strong. After all, in offering such a service you are effectively turning the marketing message into a product, as the gap between the thing promoted and the promotion itself becomes almost non-existent.

Here are some of the most common forms of premium service:

- *Information services.* If the information is useful enough, mobile users may be willing to pay for it as a premium service. Before it was paid for by sponsors, the London Underground news service Tubehell ran as a paid-for premium service.
- *Results services.* Sports results have been used as the basis of premium services.
- *Entertainment services.* The success of the Bridget Jones SMS service highlighted the potential of SMS as an entertainment medium.

As well as ensuring you have a strong service to offer, for premium services to work you also need to operate an uncomplicated payment mechanism. Reverse billing has been identified as such a mechanism for content providers. This involves content providers sharing revenues with operators.

A growing number of operator partnerships have shown how this model can work. The content provider offers the content database while the operator establishes an SMS gateway and billing system. In most cases the mobile user will request content from the operator, who in turn requests it from the content provider. Once the service has been delivered the operator bills the user and then shares the revenues with whoever provided the content. In his mobile mentor slot, Mark Fitzgerald, the Product Development Director at WAPMX, takes a closer look at the potential for reverse billing.

Case study: *Bridget Jones' Diary*

Helen Fielding, author of the best-selling homage to singledom *Bridget Jones' Diary*, launched a Bridget-based text messaging premium service with Finnish wireless entertainment provider RIOT-E. The service was launched on 13 April 2001, the day the film version of Fielding's novel – starring Renee Zellweger and Hugh Grant – was released.

It included personality tests, an 'Ask Bridget' service, *Bridget Jones' Guide to Life* and predictable obsessions on dieting and dating. In addition, it was also possible for mobile users to pay for 'diary notes' written by Bridget (of course), to be delivered to their mobile phones, personal digital assistants or e-mail inboxes. A typical message read: 'Can't believe I am starting a new year in a single bed in my parents' house. It's too humiliating.' The service was aimed at a global market (although mainly at Europe and the United States).

In a statement made at the time of the service launch, RIOT-E Chief Executive Jan Wellman said, 'Mobile is flexible, dynamic and has an immediacy which is not possible with any other medium. Bridget can text others every day to report on the progress of her bikini diet or other urgent matters.'

One of the remarkable things about this SMS campaign was Fielding's hands-on involvement. Indeed, Fielding stated that SMS was the perfect medium for the campaign, as Bridget's obsession with e-mail would have by now turned her into an 'SMS junkie'. Fielding also suggested that the nature of text is suited to Bridget's neurotic state of mind. 'You can be in communication with significant others anytime and anywhere – or not, which can be heartbreaking and obviously requires major analysis and discussion through further texting,' says Fielding.

The campaign was also significant because it came at a time when text messaging was viewed as a predominantly teenage phenomenon. When thousands of women in their late twenties and early thirties proved willing to pay for them, it confirmed that mobile marketing was relevant to mainstream, adult audiences. Within two weeks of launching, 50,000 messages were being sent on a weekly basis, resulting in £12,000 revenue per week. The combination of the right content, provided at exactly the right time, proved just how successful premium services could be.

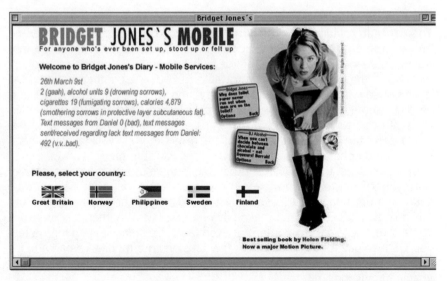

Figure 3.1   The neurotic Bridget takes time to text thousands of subscribers

Mobile mentor: Mark Fitzgerald, Product Development Director, WAP MX

Reverse billing SMS: the future of micro payment and saviour of m-commerce?

The uptake of SMS as a consumer technology has been a phenomenal success by any measure. While many have been astonished by it, some of those in the camp believing that connectivity, rather than content, is king claim to have predicted it. Like fixed-line telephones, e-mail and mobile telephones before it, SMS provides people with another creative way to do what they like doing best: interacting with each other. Only this time, since the network effect with mobile phones had already happened, SMS simply piggybacked onto a proven, successful platform.

As user–user texting has soared, businesses have looked on hungrily for opportunities to earn a piece of the action. Until recently many have been confined to experiment with SMS marketing as just another channel. Meanwhile, content owners have relied either on advertising to earn a fee for delivering their wares (such as ringtones and logos) or, more clumsily, on ancillary payment methods such as premium rate numbers.

However, the maturing SMS market has unleashed a category-killing technology on a world primed to embrace it with open arms: reverse billing SMS. The concept couldn't be simpler. In response to a user request, a service provider sends out an SMS for which it can bill the user a price of its choosing. It's instantaneous, painless and, unlike high rate numbers, uses a technology with which the user is entirely comfortable. In 2001 the content provider was disillusioned with having to provide everything for free on the Internet and worried about the increasing consumer cynicism and distant, uncertain revenue opportunities from 3G. Now, at last, content providers around the world can start to generate immediate revenue from willing consumers, whom the prophets of doom said would never want to pay.

Don't mistake this as just another fad either, useful for those cheeky purveyors of ringtones and logos. Consumers are tucking into all sorts of content, from finance to football. Just as exciting is the application of the technology as a complete micro-payment facility. Whether it's premium content on the Web, 3G content or even (as in Scandinavia) parking meters you want to pay for, no problem. A few taps on your mobile keypad and it's on your phone bill a few seconds later. As our clients are demonstrating, imagination is the limit.

This is good news for everybody and should ensure that SMS is here to stay. The visible cash generation from reverse billing is keeping the momentum going as new technologies come online, and giving a much needed boost to the world of m-commerce.

WAP MX is a specialist in the field of wireless technology, its main aim being to provide specialist wireless IT services to various corporate clients.

Paid content PC problems

Many mobile marketers may be deterred from charging for content because of lessons learnt from the dot.com fallout. For those with a stake in the desktop Internet, paid content is, to say the least, a sore point. Up until 2002 almost all content has been free online and companies have not been able to charge consumers for it. In fact, 'adult' sites have been the only type of online business that generates significant income from paid content. Of the millions spent on content by Western European Internet users in 2001, a staggering 70 per cent was spent on adult content, with the rest being generated mainly from games, finance and business news.

While media businesses are launching paid content initiatives across Europe, consumers are still very reluctant to pay for content on their PC. According to a Jupiter MMXI 2002 survey, 47 per cent of

European Web users would not even consider paying for content on the PC Internet in the future. (However, 16 per cent of Europeans would consider paying for music online, a much higher percentage than other categories.)

It is expected that the majority of future consumer spending on paid content will come from broadband-related content which benefits from faster speed and 'always on' features. (In the Jupiter survey, 67 per cent of total European paid content spending will come from music, gaming, and online video in 2006.)

However, the researchers predict that although a gradually growing number of PC users will pay for content, the vast majority of the Internet will remain free and there will not be a dramatic shift from a free to a paid Internet, especially among narrowband users. The only companies that will generate solid paid content revenues on the PC will be the ones that offer entertainment-related content.

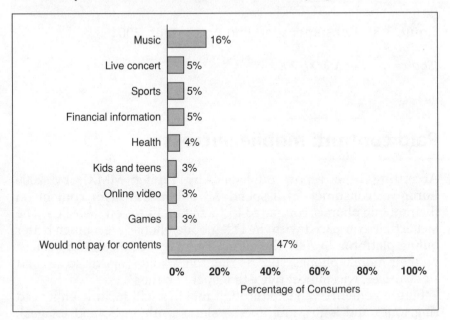

European Internet Users Who Consider Paying for Content

Figure 3.2   European Internet users who consider paying for content

(Source: Jupiter MMXI, 2002)

Consumer Spending on Content 2001–2006

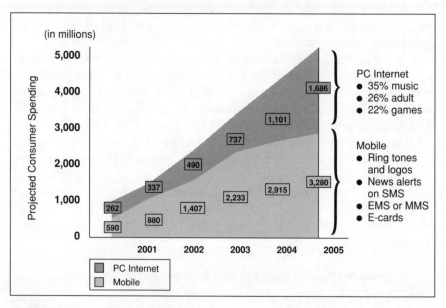

Figure 3.3   Consumer spending on content, 2001

(Source: Jupiter MMXI, 2002)

Paid content: mobile success

According to a report published by Jupiter MMXI, by 2006 European consumers will spend 3.3 billion Euros for content on their mobile phones, compared to 1.7 billion Euros on their PCs. The fact is that, compared with the PC, mobile phones are a much better billing platform. In 2001, the money spent by Europeans for content on their mobile phones, such as ring tones, logos, sports scores and stock prices, was almost twice that spent on the PC.

Future content available through mobiles will include enhanced ring tones and logos, multimedia alerts (with audio and images), and electronic greeting cards. This last phenomenon in particular indicates the PC/mobile difference. For instance, Jupiter MMXI states that while electronic greeting cards will remain a popular, mostly free service on the Web, consumers will actually pay for them on their mobile phones, as they have been paying for ring-tones and logo downloads.

'Increasing usage of short messaging service on mobile phones is good news for the media industry,' says Olivier Beauvillain, author of the Jupiter report. 'Newspapers and magazines struggling to generate direct consumer revenues from their Web sites have more opportunity to charge for content on mobile phones. They should use their Web presence as a way to promote mobile content with which they will be able to generate more revenues.' Ultimately the Internet, particularly the PC variety, is expected to be free in a way in which mobile services are not.

Competitions

One of the most popular forms of mobile marketing, particularly text-message-based marketing, is competitions. Pepsi, Sony and McDonald's are just three of the major global brands to have used entry into a competition as an incentive to become a part of their text message database.

Coca-Cola has also caught onto the value of SMS competitions, combining individual passwords (printed inside bottle caps) with SMS. This enables coke drinkers to instantly determine if they have won prizes. Smaller companies too, such as Irish-drinks company The Brew Crew, have also implemented successful text competitions. (The incentive for The Brew Crew campaign was to win a free keg of beer.)

The main advantage competitions have as the basis of a text messaging campaign is that the prize provides users with a tangible reason to contact the relevant company. The more attractive the prize is to the target audience, the higher the chance of success. If there is a disadvantage, it is the fact that competitions, by their very nature, are normally set within a limited timescale. Once the mobile user has registered, the opportunities for a two-way exchange can be equally limited. The key thing is to ensure that the entrant has the option of receiving news of future competitions and other promotions.

In order to extend the initial opportunities for two-way interaction, some campaigns have used a quiz format. This means that after the user has signed up, questions can be sent at regular intervals. After a certain number of questions, typically five, participants are told whether or not they have answered correctly. It is normally at this crucial stage that they are invited to opt in to receive more promotions. Provided the quiz has been fun and relevant, the target mobile user will normally choose to opt in. This is because ongoing interaction has already occurred and, from the user's standpoint, the risk factor often associated with subscribing to a text message marketing service has been lowered.

As well as quiz-based competitions, role-playing games have also proven to be an effective way of attracting prize-hungry mobile users. One of the first role-play campaigns to kick-start this trend was created to promote the film *Planet of the Apes*. Mobile users who had opted in to the database were sent a text message offering them the chance to win a prize if they could defeat the apes. The game was launched by an outbound message, whereby users had to press 1 on their keypad as quickly as possible to kill the attacking ape. This 'fastest finger first' format has since been replicated in a variety of text message competitions, particularly those aimed at a youth market.

Figure 3.4 The Brew Crew discovered the key to motivating mobile users: free beer

Reasons to run a competition

As mentioned above, competitions provide mobile users with a great incentive to make contact with a company. Outlined below are some of the more specific reasons to run a competition:

● *To launch a service.* One of the reasons to create a text message competition is that it provides a great way to launch a service, particularly a mobile one. For instance, First Choice Holidays, one of Europe's leading tour operators, ran an SMS competition to launch its mobile booking service. In this particular case, all entrants had to do was text a designated code and number, then answer one simple trivia question.

● *To build a database.* A strong incentive, particularly a strong cash incentive, is needed if you are to add new users to your database.

● *To limit opt-outs.* By providing your established pool of subscribers with the chance to win a prize, you will also be limiting the number of subscribers wanting to opt out.

How to make a text competition a success

When trying to maximize a competition's chances of success, the first question you need to ask yourself is, 'What do I want to achieve?' In some cases, an SMS competition will be used as an end in itself, serving simply as a promotional exercise and a way of capturing the public's imagination. Often, however, SMS competitions are used as a means of building a database of opt-in subscribers. In such cases, the prize is intended to 'incentivize' mobile users into an SMS relationship with a company.

Whatever the reason is for creating an SMS competition, there are certain guidelines to follow in order to receive the desired response:

● *Have a good prize.* As mentioned above, the better the prize, the higher the level of interest is likely to be. When the TSB Bank became the first Irish retail bank to interact with its target customers using an SMS-based competition, it realized the prize offered had to be equally monumental. A free 'trip around the world' was offered to the participants who managed to answer every question right and provide the best response to a tie-breaker.

- *Have a cross-media approach.* SMS competitions have been shown to work best in conjunction with other media. Outdoor advertising in particular has managed to generate high response rates, possibly because it targets users when they are free to use their mobile (at bus stops, train stations etc).
- *Be imaginative.* Imaginative competitions are always more likely to have a 'viral' effect, encouraging mobile users to spread the word. The *Guardian's* SMS Poetry Competition provides a good example of how a bit of imagination can go a long way.
- *Make it relevant.* A competition needs to be not only imaginative, but also relevant to your target audience. After all it's not the number of entrants that counts, but the number of entrants who are likely to be interested in your business and the products it has to offer.
- *Make it last.* As mentioned above, multiple-stage quizzes enable you to build up some form of SMS relationship with your customers before inviting them to receive further promotions.
- *Make it timely.* Think of the time of year your message should run. Could it have a Christmas, Valentine's or summer holiday theme? Also, think about the time of day you should send the competition messages out. For the TSB 'Dnt tlk just txt us' campaign, students were targeted not only via their favourite communication media (the mobile phone), but also at the best time of the day – during commuting hours.

Coupons

One way marketers have added value to text message campaigns is by turning their message into a usable coupon. By making the message do something, marketers are able to ensure mobile users understand why they have been contacted. Furthermore, coupons can help to create a feeling of exclusivity, especially when used as a perk for a 'text club'. After all, there is a considerable difference between a message telling someone about a general promotion, and a message that actually activates an offer.

The most common mobile coupon or voucher is a straightforward text message that has to be shown at the point of sale. Depending on the value of the coupon, security features such as a special validation code are sometimes incorporated in order to make sure it is the genuine article. In particular, retailers can benefit from coupon-based campaigns, using them to add value to a loyalty programme. Mobile vouchers work best when sent out at relevant times. For instance, a discount voucher for chocolates and flowers would work particularly well the day before Valentine's Day. Obviously, the more you know about the members of your database (in terms of age, gender, location, lifestyle) the more tailored coupons can be. Adding a time limit to the offer is also a good idea, given the immediacy of the medium.

With the advent of improved location-based services, the role of coupons for mobile marketing looks set to be even more important. However, no matter how good the offer is you are making, the same rules regarding spam and over-sending messages apply here.

According to mobile service provider Brand2Hand, future enhancements to mobile coupons include the possibility of transmitting a scannable bar code as an image file to the handset. However, this depends on a common standard being adopted by mobile manufacturers.

As mentioned elsewhere in this book, mobile coupons are great for building loyalty, but they are rarely enough of an incentive in themselves for mobile users to subscribe to a campaign. In most cases, an additional, immediate incentive is required, such as a downloadable game or competition entry.

Generally, mobile coupons fall into one of two categories. Impulse coupons are highly time-sensitive coupons designed by marketers to increase impulse purchases. Typically, impulse coupons are sent to subscribers who have opted in, but are unaware when they will receive them. Preselected coupons have, as their name suggests, been preselected by subscribers who have expressed an interest in certain products. They are typical as part of a long-term loyalty programme.

Tickets

In addition to coupons, mobile tickets are also growing in popularity. For instance, the Virgin-owned London nightclub Heaven uses mTicket, a UK-based mobile ticketing system, in order to distribute tickets via mobile devices. The system enables club-goers with mobile tickets to jump the club's notoriously long queue. All they then need to do is show the bouncer the password displayed on their mobile screen. Ministry of Sound is also planning a mobile ticketing scheme alongside VIP passes and queue jumpers.

ClubConnexion, the dance community Web site, offers mobile ticketing services to its users. The incentive for users is that, as well as enabling them to jump the queue, they are included on a discounted paying guest list. As SMS is not perfectly suited to lengthy information gathering, ClubConnexion invites users to submit their details, including mobile number, to the site. The ticket numbers, along with the booking confirmation, are then sent via SMS to the user.

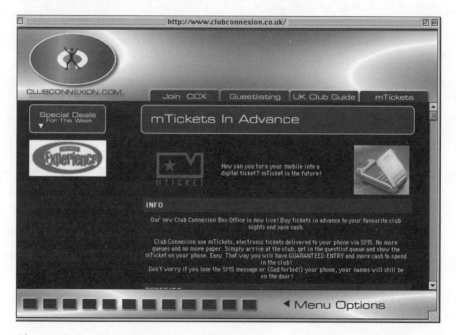

Figure 3.5   Texters can buy their tickets via ClubConnexion

According to ClickZ columnist and co-author of *Clicks, Bricks and Brands*, Martin Lindstrom, this is just the beginning. 'Imagine the convenience of being able to carry your train or airline tickets as m-tickets,' he told readers of his column. As with coupons, mobile tickets activate the message and enable users to act upon it.

Location, location, location

Location-based services are one of the stickiest subjects related to mobile marketing. Depending on who you believe, they represent a consumer utopia or a dystopian nightmare. First, let's take a look at the consumer utopia. This is where you let your phone contact you with news of only those local offers you are really looking for, saving you the chore of traipsing around the shops for hours. The only problem with this scenario is that, to really tell you what you want, the phone needs not only to know your location, but also read your mind. To imagine the potential nightmare, think of walking down Oxford Street full of shops equipped with location-sensitive services. How many alerts would it take before your beloved mobile device met a sorry end under the wheels of a Number 25 bus? Five? Ten? Two hundred and sixty?

The threat of spam and 'text overload' is therefore increased with the rise in location-based services. Even if mobile users have opted in to receive alerts, they may soon get frustrated if they are alerted every time they walk by the relevant location.

That said, some location-based services have proved very popular. For instance, the ZagMe opt-in service, which runs in two UK shopping centres, has over 50,000 willing subscribers receiving news of money-saving offers. Brainstorm (see below) provides another example. However, perhaps the most useful location services may be outside the retail arena. The London Tubehell service shows one way in which location-based services could win over the sceptics. Tubehell uses SMS alerts to keep subscribers up to date about delays and problems on their daily route. Such a service, rather than hassling users, actually reduces the hassle of everyday life by providing exactly the sort of information people need to know.

Case study: location-based shopping

In September 2000, Saverfone (since acquired by Brainstorm) launched the UK's first location-based shopping service for retailers and brands to reach target audiences all over the country.

Embracing cutting edge technologies, the service works with merchants nationwide to provide consumers with a database of special offers.

Here is how it works. Shoppers access the database, which is organized by location and retail category, via WAP, text messaging or the Web. (They are not charged for this service.) With thousands of retail outlets showing thousands of simultaneous promotions, the service offers marketers what Brainstorm refers to as 'a truly ground-breaking way of precisely targeting consumers with relevant offers when they are in the immediate vicinity of the store'.

The media response to the service has been especially favourable. *Incentive Business* said that it 'raises for the first time the prospect of precisely targeted online one-to-one marketing,' while the *Sunday Express* told its readers they no longer have to traipse around the shops looking for the best bargains. As Brainstorm CEO Steve Wunker pointed out, 'we don't spam anybody – this is a permission-based marketing tool so consumers are both protected and in control'. According to *Direct Marketing Week*, 'it is easy to see that this win-win situation is an absolute "must have" in the retailers' marketing armoury'.

Alerts

Alerts, which can be either location or time sensitive (or both), fit perfectly with the mobile media. After all, mobile devices are carried around by people wherever they go, and enable marketers to reach users at any time. Although they should always operate on a permission-based model, text message alerts are essentially a push-based service. They therefore work well with other, pull-based forms of mobile marketing activity. Lycos, the Web portal and search engine, offers shopping alerts via SMS. 'As a push-based service, the SMS shopping alerts complement the SMS price comparison tool we're also offering,' explains Lycos UK's Managing Director, Alex Kovach.

As we have seen, Brainstorm is one company offering marketers an SMS sales alert service, allowing advertisers to push details of promotions via SMS to interested users who have signed up for the system either using a Web or WAP form, or by sending a text message. Significantly, Brainstorm's service enables users to specify the maximum number of text messages to be sent weekly, and preferred time of day for delivery.

As well as for sales purposes, alerts can also be used to deliver timely information such as stock quotes, sports results, business news or earth-shattering gossip. They can also be used in conjunction with a chat-based service.

In August 2001, 'youth lifestyle empire' the Ministry of Sound used alerts for its mammoth Knebworth01 event. 'When you are staging an event of this size there will always be late additions,' explained Ministry of Sound's Creative Director at the time the alerts were announced:

> There is a significant feel good factor in being the first to know, and Brand2Hand [the company which set up the MoS alert system] delivers it. In the days leading up to the event at Knebworth we had two very important additions to the line up. We used the alerts twice to let the membership know. At the late stage of these updates we could not have reached them all in any other way.

Sponsorships

Another way marketers can reach mobile users is by sponsoring an already established messaging service. The benefits here are obvious. Firstly, although it costs money, the headache of implementing a campaign is alleviated. Furthermore, the risk factor is reduced. Instead of hoping for the best, marketers can attach themselves to a service that has already proved successful. In fact, the very act of sponsorship can make a text messaging service even more popular. The sponsorship money can be used to add value to the service or reduce costs for customers. As we have discussed, before being funded through sponsorship, the Tubehell SMS alert originally operated on a paying model.

In order for the sponsorship to be a success, it is necessary to ensure the service is relevant to your company or brand. For instance, it would make perfect sense for a health food supplier to sponsor a text message diet service. It would not be such a good idea for a chocolate bar manufacturer to do the same (unless of course, it was a low calorie chocolate bar). It is also a good idea to look for a service that enables you to target specific users and which has a strong understanding of who subscribes to the service. For instance, Tubehell is able to tell its sponsors that 92 per cent of users live within Greater London and that 75 per cent are between the ages of 22 and 31. Users can also be targeted right down to their tube station, age and sex among other criteria.

Sponsorships are also among the most successful forms of WAP marketing and, indeed, Internet marketing in general.

Mobile payment services

As mobile phones increasingly become 'life support devices', it is perhaps inevitable that we will end up not only paying for mobile services, but also paying through them. Mobile phones that double as wallets have long been talked about. Now, however, they are a reality. Everything from a soft drink to an airline ticket can potentially be paid for via a mobile device.

Orange established its first mobile payment service in Denmark. Vodafone runs a UK micropayments service and has trailed an M-Wallet mobile payment system in various European countries. Manufacturers have also been driving the concept forward. Nokia's 6340 phone, launched in Spring 2002, enables users to store, encrypt and secure credit card information within the phone's memory. These details can then be transferred to WAP sites.

M-payment, which is expected to be used primarily in areas such as ticketing and entertainment, will take a while for people (consumers and marketers) to get used to. The lack of a single m-payment standard could also hinder development, but already we have seen innovative examples of m-payment in action. For instance, Irish firm Mobile 2 Meter enables car owners to pay for their parking tickets via WAP. Mobile micropayments are expected to be used in conjunction with MP3 technology so mobile users can pay for music through their phone.

If you have registered with the Paybox mobile payment service you can even cover lunch at Soho's Circus restaurant with an m-payment. After you have finished your meal, you give the waiter your mobile phone and he calls Paybox's voice response service to give it to them. Paybox automatically calls you, and asks you to type in your PIN and authorize the bill. (I have actually given this service a go – it works. Good food, too.) However, most mobile payments still arise from premium rated text messages or reverse booking.

Mobile channels

Mobile channels, or advertising networks, enable marketers to reach consumers who have signed up to receive text messages in return for a small incentive. For instance, The Mobile Channel (www.themobilechannel.co.uk) enables subscribers to get electronic top-ups for their phone cards, high street vouchers or charity donations. They then receive a maximum of three commercial messages a day from different brands. However, as they do not always know which brands they will be contacted by, the effectiveness of mobile channels for marketers is debatable. Targeting is normally limited to broad classifications such as age and gender.

That said, if a marketer chooses a mobile channel to distribute downloadable coupons, it makes it possible for networks to build a pricing scheme based on actual rate. For instance, advertisers on the Vindigo (www.vindigo.com) network only pay if prospects are converted into customers.

Figure 3.6 Vindigo offers location-specific content delivered direct to mobiles

---

Mobile mentor: Mark Selby, Founder, MobileChannel Network

Content, context and community must be on the menu

Mobile marketing has enormous potential, enabling the delivery of targeted, effective messages to specific individuals, wherever they are, on devices that are with them all day. The messages are almost certain to be read by the recipient. Furthermore, the opportunities to establish a dialogue with these individuals are considerable. Many well-known consumer brands have now experimented with the mobile medium. Unfortunately, many have had limited success. The reasons vary but common threads include brevity of campaigns, poor recipient segmentation, weak editorial/creatives, lack of follow-up or support through other media, and lack of clear opt-in and opt-out procedures.

Content, context and community remain three critical elements for effective mobile marketing. Content must be structured in such a manner that the valued elements are not diminished by over-intrusive marketing messages. Services must contextually reflect the lifestyle and interests of recipients; the user experience should be one that recipients want to share within their specific communities and act upon. The community strategy should seek to leverage a twist on Metcalfe's law, namely that the value, usefulness, or utility, of the network (community) equals the square of the number of users.

SMS has been available, and used, for a long time. Yet many of the consumer brands that have experimented with it appear to derive more satisfaction from the fact they have actually used it for mobile marketing than from benchmarking the effectiveness of their campaigns against others. As we enter the EMS, MMS and 3G environments we can anticipate further examples of this behaviour, with individuals blind-sided by the novelty of technology rather than the intrinsic value of the mobile medium for marketing.

Coming to terms with this medium will take time. The risk is that poor marketing, widespread spamming and user frustration could significantly diminish its potential value. Rather than take these routes, it is essential that learning is drawn from elsewhere, including CRM and direct marketing techniques, experience engineering and attention economics, to name but a few. It is not simply a case of building a list of mobile phone numbers and sending 160-character text messages to them.

Mobile Channel.Network delivers original and unique content services to mobile devices. The company develops and supplies specific technologies to support the delivery of content services. Among other projects, it worked with Nokia to deliver an SMS and WAP-based service for the Sydney Olympics.

The best text you've ever had

According to the rather worn out marketing cliché, if you really want to sell a product, sell it with sex. If you can, to paraphrase the famous Heineken strapline, make your campaign get to the parts other marketers cannot reach, then you may be onto a winner. The popularity of dating and flirting SMS services might indicate that adding a bit of sauce to the marketing menu is the way to go.

However, as mobile marketing success hinges on relevancy, following the 'sex route' is inadvisable for most businesses. Furthermore, given the highly sensitive nature of the mobile medium, messages with even slightly risqué content could be considered as unwelcome, and therefore as spam (even if the mobile user has asked for them in the first place). The fact that it can be difficult to find out the age of every mobile user means even greater problems can arise.

That said, sexy text messages can work where they are relevant to the product or brand promoted. For instance, *Cosmopolitan*, the best-selling magazine for 'feisty females', ran a text messaging service providing subscribers with a daily tip on how to have the best orgasm ever. Readers were able to receive the service by texting the word 'orgasm' to a special number printed in the highly popular magazine. An extra incentive to sign up for the service was provided with a competition to win a gambling holiday in Las Vegas – with £10,000 prize money. The 'sex' element certainly helped increase the viral marketing potential of the campaign. 'I've got no doubt that a lot of these tips will be forwarded onto partners to help refresh their memories,' said Gary Andersen-Jones, Managing Director of Quartez, the company which pro-vided the sophisticated text messaging system for the *Cosmopolitan* campaign. When asked to comment on why this approach works, Andersen said that 'text messaging has never been more popular – mix this with sex and money, and we have to have a winner'.

Although research has found that 'flirty' texts are among the most popular form of person-to-person messaging, it is still unwise to send out risqué messages unless you can be sure that all your subscribers will be, ahem, receptive.

Last word

Mobile marketing offers companies a broader menu of campaign options than almost any other medium. For all the possibilities of the PC-based Internet, the standard Web has let marketers down on certain counts. For instance, Internet users, in the main, are not willing to pay for content. Mobile users, on the other hand, expect to pay for quality information sent to their devices.

However, although the range of options may have widened, the stakes have been raised. Whichever mobile marketing route you decide to follow, you need to make sure it will help, not hinder, your brand development. It is important to realize that what may look like a fantastic avenue for bringing in extra revenue could degenerate into a marketing cul-de-sac. To ensure this does not happen, make sure that you understand the new hierarchy. Not only do consumers have the power to reject marketing messages, they also have the power not to receive them in the first place. Everything is on their terms.

four

Two-way marketing

A mobile phone is still used primarily for one thing: communication; two-way communication, to be exact. It makes sense then, for companies to incorporate a two-way aspect within any mobile marketing campaign. As Dan Pelson states in his mobile mentor slot in this chapter, 'there is a fortune to be made in providing utility with one-to-one, one-to-few, and one-to-many communication'.

However, the growth in mobile communications networks and channels also means that consumers are more connected than ever before. While this can be a force for good, marketers need to understand the way this has changed the whole nature of marketing. This change, which started slowly with the rise of the Internet, is now starting to accelerate.

A two-way medium

Mobile marketing is not just about using new technology, but requires a completely new way of thinking. Not only does it require you to be open to different avenues of marketing communication, it also requires a more flexible attitude generally. The most essential thing to realize is that this is a two-way medium. Customer response to campaigns should be welcome because it may lead to a deeper understanding of your audience. After all, this could be the first opportunity your customers have had to talk back to you. It is important to respect the dialogue you have initiated by listening to what they have to say.

Mobile marketing also ups the ante. With print, television, radio, Web and outdoor campaigns, it can often be enough just to aim for increased brand or product awareness. A giant billboard may clutter the landscape, but it is inherently less intrusive than a short line of text sent directly to a person's mobile phone. A message which essentially says 'Hi! Remember us? We're fantastic!' is simply not going to work via this medium. Every single message you send out must be of real value to each recipient. This may take a lot of time and effort, it may even take a lot of money, but ultimately this customer-centric focus is necessary in order to establish profitable relationships via mobile marketing. Below, Brand2Hand's Richard Lander takes a more in-depth look at the way the mobile medium impacts on customer relationship management.

Mobile mentor: Richard Lander, Marketing Manager, Brand2Hand

Mobile CRM

Building effective mobile CRM projects requires some adjustments to the set of values from an Internet or intranet CRM project. Working with SMS helps you build up sensitivities to the medium.

SMS is much more personal and immediate for the end user than many other forms of electronic communication. One of the things that keeps SMS so alive, ironically, is the limit to the size of the message. Each SMS message is like one 'breath', you read it from end to end as a single quantum. SMS arrives in your pocket, and follows you everywhere.

Identity is a key component of CRM systems. Having worked on plenty of conventional CRM projects before getting into SMS, I found that there were a lot of things to 'un-learn' before I could get to the right mindset to work with SMS. Typical CRM system planning is all about tracking, designing, modelling, testing, manipulating and indexing identity, contact data, company/individual relationships, preferences, postcodes and people. There is a lot of data and even more data structure in a typical CRM application.

Keeping track of identity is also important with an SMS CRM campaign, but things happen at a different level. The most important pieces of information are the context of the communication and the telephone number that we are communicating with. Additional information is a bonus, and we often need it in particular situations, but there are a lot of very worthwhile CRM applications with SMS where all we know about a person is that they responded to a particular campaign by texting in from their phone. We know the number, and the context, and that is enough.

When we link SMS to the Web, through conventional registration or logo downloads, then the opportunity exists to gather more structured information. Resist the temptation to tie up your user in three screens of registration data. It's a waste of time, and a waste of their goodwill. Most likely you will lose them in the process, and that's the end of a beautiful and potentially profitable relationship. Stick to the bare bones. If you want to give people region-specific information, ask for their post code. We often ask for age and sex too, as it does help to build a better idea of who you are dealing with, but stick to the bare minimum.

The cleanest CRM that we do has nothing but the phone number that the user texted us with, the time and date, and the content of the response. The content could be a single word. From this data we can gather enough information to work out the right dialogues and responses. People who responded very quickly might be the early adopters. People who have responded more than once are extra keen. You can infer habits from the time and date that the message comes in, and use the time that they texted in as a likely time to get a receptive response on a return message. That way you don't wake up late birds with an early text, or vice versa.

SMS, being so short, encourages a two way dialogue. We often build up SMS campaigns to follow a dialogue, which we can then program in to autoresponses. Simple ones are like this:

Text FITWORLD with your name on 07xxx 123 123 to register. The first 100 people to text us will win a free sports bag.

So then the first 100 people get a message saying:

Congratulations – you have won a free FITWORLD sports bag. Reply with your full address and we will mail it to you.

Once the first 100 have contacted you the message changes to:

Hi – you are registered for FITWORLD. Watch this space for FITWORLD news and special events. Text back UNSUBSCRIBE to leave.

More complex dialogues can go like this:

MONSTER2 – the sequel – is back, visit WWW.MONSTER2.COM.

On the Web site:

Register here for interest in the film, for previews and special promotions.

Once registered you can text all of the people in Glasgow, and say:

We have a special pre-screening of Monster2 with 100 pairs of tickets available this Saturday. If you would like a pair of tickets reply: TICKETS.

The 'TICKETS' responses get a reply:

Here is your ticket for Monster2. Admit 2. Please bring this message with you to the door. This Saturday 5pm. Central Cinema. A42-C33-T54.

Once you have run out of tickets you say:

Sorry – tickets for the pre-screening are all gone. When the film is released show this message and get two tickets for the price of one: C44-A19-G51.

For ticket holders you can then send a reminder:

Reminder – tonight you have two tickets for Monster2. 5pm, Central Cinema. Enjoy the show!

After the show you can also say:

Hope you enjoyed Monster2. Please text back any comments you have and rate the film out of 10. We really value your opinion.

Mention SMS and CRM in the same sentence and you are starting to suffer from three letter acronym overload (TLAO). When we refer to CRM in the context of SMS we normally think of CONSUMER Relationship Management. A lot of the dialogue is pre-purchase, so you hope that these people will become customers, and SMS is well suited for B2C, as well as B2B relationships.
    London-based Brand2Hand offers a marketing and customer communication system, using SMS text and graphics to mobile phones.

Connected markets

The information age is characterized not only by an excess of data, but also by an increased connectivity. As the authors of *The Cluetrain Manifesto* have warned, markets are becoming more connected every single day. The excessive speed with which Internet services such as Hotmail became widely popular testify to this 'network effect', as does the whole concept of viral marketing. Whether or not, as legend has it, the founders of Hotmail literally woke up one morning to discover half of Sweden had subscribed to their service, the fact the story was believed at all indicates the evident power of hyperconnected markets.

According to *Cluetrain* co-author Doc Searls, 'the Internet is a powerful demonstration of a pure market conversation at work'. With the mobilization of the Internet, coupled with the irrepressible rise of text messaging, the 'market conversation' is even more active. And if, as Searls suggests, 'conversation is the sound of the market where creators and customers are close enough to feel each other's heat,' then now the temperature has been raised further.

Although the fixed Internet – through discussion boards, e-mail and consumer Web sites – has brought consumers together, its conversational power looks set to be shadowed by the rise of mobile communications, and text messaging in particular. We, as marketers, need to appreciate the fact that we are no longer communicating into a void. If marketers take short cuts and fail to think from the mobile user's perspective, there may be a heavy price to pay. If, however, they are willing to engage in conversation, and to learn from the market rather than preach to it, then the rewards can be great. Ultimately, word travels fast, whether good or bad.

For anyone still in doubt about the connecting power of text messaging, it is worth taking a look at the Philippines, where SMS has become central to the way of life. In January 2001 an SMS message was passed on from person to person, asking them to show their support at an anti-government demonstration. An incredible 2 million people turned up to show their disapproval. The government collapsed shortly afterwards.

Getting personal

Two-way marketing involves communicating with consumers on their own terms. But what are these terms? Well, first and foremost, marketers need to have respect for the intimate nature of mobile communication. If nothing else, they must acknowledge that mobile phones are personal devices.

Generally speaking, mobile users do not care about technology. What they do care about is why they use it: namely, to interact with their friends, colleagues and family. When they are not being used for the purposes of interaction, mobiles serve to fill those rare and precious times of the day when people have nothing else to do but play a game or access useful content. Either way, people are using this medium in a way they use no other. The mobile device is carried with people at all times, wherever they travel. It can provide a lifeline to people when no other form of contact is available. In other words a mobile device is about as up close and personal as a marketer can get to potential customers, short of making face-to-face contact (and besides, many mobile users now prefer communicating via SMS to doing so in person). In order to use this medium effectively, marketers must understand this uniquely personal element.

According to Sep Riahi, Lastminute.com's Vice President of Business Development, businesses can no longer escape this issue. 'We certainly view personalization as the next major step forward,' he says. 'The time-sensitive nature of our business means it will be vital to us to ensure that information is highly targeted and relevant to the individual customer. In future, those businesses which do not work on this basis will risk alienating consumers.'

Personalization does not mean, however, that all messages should start with the recipient's name. Given the 160-character limit of most SMS messages this is often impractical. What it does mean, is communicating to people in a way that is relevant to them. How can this relevancy be gauged? First and foremost, by the subscription process itself. If someone has subscribed to receive information, alerts or coupons regarding a certain service, the message rarely requires further personalization.

The key thing is for marketers not to overstate their case. In order to build up their database some companies could be tempted to offer more than they can deliver. While this approach will make up the numbers in the short term, it will do them no favours in the long term, as consumers start to distrust what they have to say.

Obviously the more choices and pre-selectable criteria you can provide at the beginning, the easier it will be to personalize your service. Again, mobile marketers may have something to learn here from some of their Internet counterparts. For instance, when Borders.com decided to create an e-mail newsletter they realized they had something of a problem. How could they personalize it to their customers' highly disparate tastes? After all, who is a typical Borders customer?

What they did was to scrap the idea of sharing one newsletter, and instead they created nine, each aimed at a different type of subscriber. There's a Business Class newsletter full of financial and market information, a Digital Cinema newsletter aimed at the growing army of DVD devotees, Borders Alchemy for those interested in science and philosophy, and so on. Subscribers are therefore able to personalize the service simply by signing up to it. Mobile marketers, especially those with a broad range of products and services, should think along similar lines and avoid the 'one size fits all' approach.

Market research

Owing to its two-way nature, text messaging has emerged as a useful market research tool. Indeed, for marketing activity which requires SMS responses from mobile users, research is conducted automatically as the campaign progresses. Sometimes, however, more in-depth research is required.

Separate SMS text surveys have been set up by mobile marketing agencies, for clients to carry out market research among their customers. For instance, 2cv:research, a youth market research agency, established a new text message survey method called txtsurvey. As all the survey participants have opted in to receive questions, response rates are very high (averaging 70–80 per cent). Another company offering SMS market research services is Brand2Hand. 'With Brand2Hand you can run a whole research project through our automated interface,' explains Daz Jamieson, Managing Director of Brand2Hand. The Brand2Hand campaign manager lets you set up a series of actions and responses which are communicated with customers using SMS. 'Research functions have been designed into Brand2Hand from the start,' says Jamieson. 'We can deliver research survey and analysis functions straight out of the box. Nothing can beat text messages for immediate delivery, value and universal coverage. This approach accelerates the customer response process, delivering excellent accuracy and value.'

Firms can also conduct their own SMS-based research, using their database. Providing mobile users have a strong incentive to respond they will often be happy to participate. Incentives used by 2cv

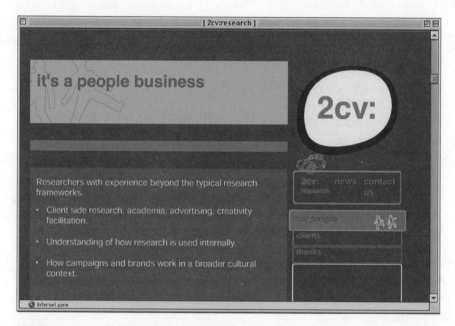

Figure 4.1   2cv is one of the leading companies offering mobile market research services

include cash credits and competition entries. Free offers and discount coupons can also be used.

The reasons why text messaging is suited to market research include:

- *Response.* The ease of response typically ensures a good return rate for surveys and questionnaires.
- *Quick results.* The speed at which the answers to text messages are delivered is extremely fast (mostly within one hour). The fact that text is such a fast-paced and immediate medium means that the whole market research process, from formulation through to assessment, can be carried out within a relatively short timeframe.
- *Open communication.* SMS's apparent ability to get people to open up and lose their inhibitions makes it perfect for quantitative research. Qualitative research, which normally requires longer responses, is less suited to text messaging. As Open University psychologist Adam Joinson has pointed out, 'when

they can't see each other, people are more focused and less concerned about being judged'.

- *Self-documentation.* The self-documenting nature of text messaging, as with e-mail, is also welcomed by market researchers.
- *Mass market research.* According to Vincent Nolan, 2cv Founder and Chairman, 'SMS is an excellent method of screening a large group'. However, unless using an external agency with a ready list of opt-in subscribers, it may take time to build your database.
- *Web compatibility.* For 2cv's txtsurvey SMS is sometimes used in conjunction with the Web. After having answered a short SMS questionnaire on their mobile phones, the txtsurvey panel are then sent a more detailed Web questionnaire to fill in. This is normally structured as multiple choice, allowing responses with just a single character message.

Text chat

SMS-based chat services have become increasingly popular, and offer marketers considerable scope for viral marketing. Chat services with a dating component, such as CosmicCupid and Mamjam, work especially well.

The secret to running a successful SMS chat service is to bring a time or location-sensitive element into the offering. One of the most famous SMS chat services is, surprisingly, based in the United States (surprising in that interoperability difficulties mean that North America is still behind in the SMS stakes). New York Celebrity Sightings enables users to send messages such as '11.30 Sarah-Jess Parker spotted in Al's Coffee House, Gren Vill'. Members therefore contribute to the group wherever and whenever they spot a star in the Big Apple. Although sceptics might suggest such a service would only attract stalkers and other unstable minds, the fact that the peer-to-peer chat element is combined with the provision of hard information has given the service mainstream appeal (not to mention media coverage).

If such a service can take off in an area with low SMS uptake, the potential for imaginative subscription-based text message chat groups elsewhere is phenomenal. Of course, the trick is to

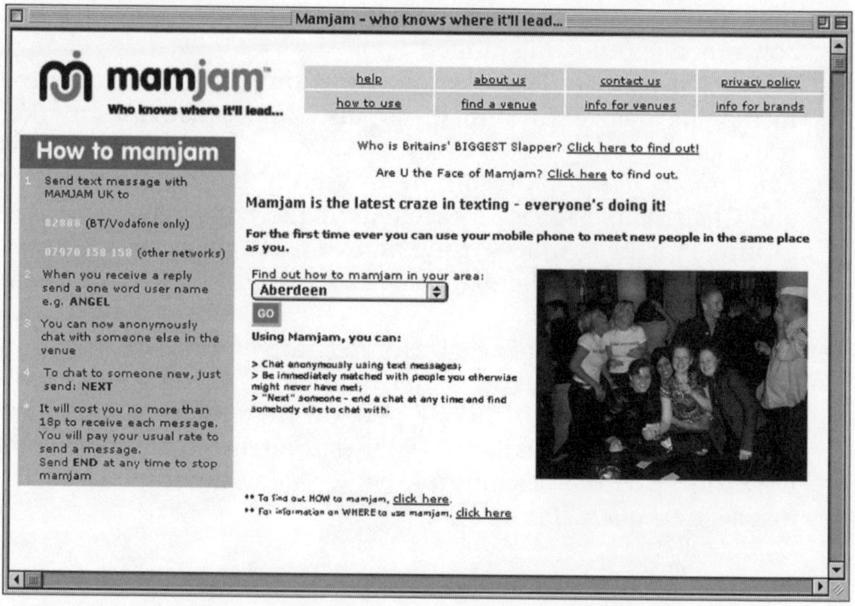

Figure 4.2   Mamjam: the flirt phenomenon

make the service relevant to your company in such a way that when subscribers chat with each other, they are in fact promoting your product or service. The other, easier, solution is to sponsor a relevant service that is already up and running.

Mobile mentor: Dan Pelson, Chairman and CEO, Bolt Inc, United States

Communication holds the key

While the SMS phenomenon in Europe and Asia has revolutionized the wireless industry, it is in many ways very simple to explain. A number of factors have to come together to make it happen, but at the root of it is simply communication. SMS is nothing more than the ability to communicate with people anytime, from any place. So what's the big deal, and why are teens and young adults such voracious users of text messaging?

Adults have had a difficult time communicating with teens for thousands of years, with both parties endlessly accusing the other of 'speaking a different language', of not listening, of not 'getting it'. The irony is that while mum and dad have a hard time getting junior to open up, teens tend to be hyper-communicators, and are constantly seeking the ability, or right, to speak their mind and get feedback. As teens go through the critical life stage when they discover who they are, open dialogue enables them to experiment with their personality and receive feedback to determine if it's acceptable to themselves and to others. Of course, the most important source of feedback is their peers, not mum and dad, not teachers, and typically not any adult. So while adults keep trying to talk to teens with little success, teens are communicating in multiple channels simultaneously at ever-increasing rates.

SMS in Europe and Asia (and the Internet in North America) has allowed this ability to communicate to explode, providing a boon to wireless carriers, often with little understanding of how they are raking in the dough. While carriers are now beginning to leverage this phenomenon to drive even greater usage of mobile devices for non-voice services, they have fallen back on what we as adults think should be the next generation of applications. This often has little to do with what the true heavy users, teens, really need: an even greater ability to communicate, and ultimately the ability to create their own peer groups, or communities, wirelessly.

Instead of focusing on 3G applications, broadband downloads of things that conjure up images of television for us old folks, and access to news/finance/sports, there is a fortune to be made in providing even more utility with one-to-one, one-to-few, and one-to-many communication. Making sense of the chaos, bringing harmony to the cacophony of ranting that occurs via messaging, is of tremendous value to consumers, even those youngsters who seem to be able to handle everything at once. While broadband applications will undoubtedly play a role in the wireless world, it will always come back to what this medium was made for: communication and communities of interest, whether that community is two people or 2,000. Traditional content as we know it will increasingly become the context for dialogue, and if the carriers are willing to understand the simplicity of it all, they will reap much greater rewards by focusing on utilities that simply drive subscriber communication.

Dan Pelson is Chairman and Chief Executive Officer of Bolt Inc., a universal communications platform for young adults that he co-founded in September 1996. Dan was the first New Economy entrepreneur to recognize the value in empowering the teen audience (estimated to reach 1.8 billion globally by 2010) and in providing marketers with an outlet to reach this critical demographic. Bolt is recognized by leading Fortune 500 companies as the partner of choice for building relationships with the youth market.

Case study: Ministry of Sound's two-way approach

Established in 1991 as a London nightclub, the Ministry of Sound has now evolved into one of the world's leading entertainment brands for young people. In addition to the club, it now has a broad range of products including record labels and a consumer magazine. Keen to stay at the forefront of both youth culture and innovative marketing, the Ministry began database marketing via text in July 2000, and now carries out regular text campaigns for its own and partner brands. One particular success which broke new ground was the S'Move text tickets campaign which was put together with mobile marketing agency Aerodeon.

When Ministry launched its new S'Move night, it represented a significant shift into a new music genre, as well as the perfect opportunity to test text messaging. According to Aerodeon the campaign objectives were to create awareness, interest and sales for the new S'Move night, and more generally to evaluate text messaging as a cost effective, two-way channel.

The Ministry's customer database included mobile phone numbers for some customers, but it was necessary to establish an easy, efficient method to supplement this. So a text registration process was created which involved inviting customers to send a text message to a phone number displayed on promotional material. This eliminated the user error inherent with traditional mechanisms, such as coupons or the Web, and meant that registrations could be sought in what Aerodeon refers to as a 'mobile lifestyle mode', such as queuing to enter the club.

Specifically, the messages were designed to be clear and to mimic the text language used by the target market. This required careful analysis of the text language abbreviations in the text messages sent to the Ministry as part of the text registration. Sending messages that closely reflect the language used by this group has been a key factor in the success of these and other youth market campaigns.

As the decision making for selecting which nightclub to attend at the weekend is consultative and tends to occur towards the end of the week, the messages were therefore targeted to arrive early evening on the weekdays preceding the S'Move night on Friday. The first two messages in particular were designed to maximize customer interaction. The first was a teaser, to arouse interest and thereby encourage a reply; the second was designed to provide more information on the S'Move night and to highlight a special offer as an additional incentive to respond. The full name was requested for authentication at the door and to enable future messages to be personalized, which is essential for any mobile marketing campaign to have the best chances of success.

All customers who responded to the second message received a text ticket, which allowed them to jump the queue if they showed the message and get in for free if they brought four friends. The message was purposefully designed to enable them to forward it to friends, thereby encouraging the marketing message to spread far beyond members of the Ministry database. The viral element, combined with the timing and careful wording, meant the level of response far exceeded expectations. In total 84 per cent of text tickets were redeemed at the door.

Figure 4.3   Ministry of Sound uses SMS to communicate with clubbers

Last word

Two-way marketing involves the ultimate challenge for any company: a loosened grip over its marketing message. However, it is only those companies willing and able to listen to their customers, and even let their customers listen to each other, who will come to appreciate how powerful marketing via mobile devices can really be.

five

Responsible marketing

Mobile devices, and the various platforms they support, amount to the most personal form of technology that has ever existed. Not only are they used by people to communicate with their nearest and dearest, but they are carried around wherever they go. This helps to explain the potential power of mobile marketing, but it is also its main problem.

People are understandably very sensitive when it comes to a device which has become such an integral part of their life. If marketers abuse the power of this medium, then the consumer backlash will be strong. Indeed, the annoyance caused by e-mail 'spam' could pale into insignificance when compared to that caused by unsolicited mobile messages.

The purpose of this chapter, including the insightful contribution from mobile mentor Jeremy Wright (the co-founder of the UK's first wireless media sales house) is to express the need for a responsible approach, and to outline the basics of what such an approach entails.

The need for responsible marketing

With the rise of mobile communications, particularly of text messaging and other non-voice based technologies, the gains for mobile marketers are potentially huge. According to the US-based Yankee Group, 26 per cent of the total wireless population will be willing to buy products, services and content subscriptions via their mobile devices by 2006. Even more optimistic was a survey conducted by the Wireless Advertising Association and ARC Group (a London-based consultancy). Nearly all of the study's respondents (more than 90 per cent) expected global mobile advertising expenditure to grow considerably over the next few years. However, the same study also found that categorized, opt-in marketing models are 'critical' if mobile marketing is to have a successful future. Furthermore, privacy concerns were seen as the biggest obstacle marketers need to tackle.

The unfortunate fact is that mobile marketing campaigns are all too often tarred with the same brush. Many significant figures, such as Web usability guru Jakob Nielsen, have come out against all forms of mobile marketing and suggest that any commercial message sent to a mobile phone goes against the interest of mobile users. However, successful mobile marketing campaigns – such as those highlighted in this book – clearly show that this is not the case. Indeed, trials in Sweden, one of the countries at the forefront of the mobile revolution, found that 76 per cent of mobile users welcome advertising so long as it is integrated within useful information services. Crucially, 28 per cent of respondents in the Swedish study (conducted by NetSurvey and Mediatude) said that the advertising they received made them interested in the campaign offer, and only 17 per cent found the advertising intrusive.

That said, other studies conducted by mobile marketing consultancies and research firms such as Cahners In-Stat have found that, while some marketers persist in sending unsolicited messages, the general view of mobile marketing will be tarnished. As Eamon Hession, a founding member of the Irish Wireless Marketing Association, points out, 'Mobile marketing will not gain public acceptance while some companies continue to send out large volumes of unsolicited SMS messages that provide no easy means for customers to opt out'. The advice the mobile experts provide is straightforward: don't abuse the trust of your actual and potential customers. Responsible marketing in this medium is even more essential than it is elsewhere, but what exactly does it involve?

According to Rachel Supple, the Business Development Director for mobile service provider iTouch, the secret to responsible wireless marketing is 'to know who and why you want to contact people'. She also says it is imperative to 'have a purpose, have their permission and collect mobile numbers of relevant customers on an ongoing basis. Do not flood the same people with different messages as this will become irritating.'

However, it is not just the quantity of messages which may prove irritating but also the manner in which they are sent. If a two-way 'conversation' is built up between the mobile user and the mobile marketer then there is less risk of overstepping the mark. 'Mobile marketers should provide an engaging marketing concept and message on mobile devices that encourages the recipient to participate in the interaction and can demonstrate clear doing so,' says John Farmer, a co-founder of SMS service and application provider Carbon Partners. 'Interaction is the key to the effective use of mobile marketing, but initiating this should be at the request of the customer.'

The spam problem

Particular care is required on the part of marketers, given the way people use and view their mobile devices. 'The mobile is a distinctly personal device and care must be taken to respect this factor – intrusive use of overt marketing messages will potentially be more damage than good,' warns Farmer. Indeed, because of this personal factor, mobile spam could prove to be an even greater nuisance than its e-mail counterpart.

In Europe and Asia, various unscrupulous companies have bought and sold lists of mobile numbers in order to send out text messages en masse to unwitting mobile users. In the United States, mobile users are even less tolerant of spam than their European and Asian counterparts. For them, mobile spam is not just an annoyance but an expense, as they usually have to pay to receive, as well as send, SMS messages. Having racked up huge bills receiving calls from marketers who have contacted them without warning, consumers have felt justifiably outraged and even called for tighter government controls. 'The economics of spam are compelling,' says Mobile Marketing Association (MMA) Chairman Steve Wunker. 'Although SMS spam is a limited problem at present, we as an industry have to crack down on the problem before it really gets started. Otherwise the whole medium will be tainted.'

In actual fact, the crackdown has already been initiated with the

MMA leading the way. In 2001 the MMA, which has over 30 members within the industry, issued a comprehensive code of practice which categorically banned the use of spam. The organization also advises great caution when renting lists of mobile numbers. Some people, such as Mobile Active's Chief Information Officer Ronnie Forbes, even go so far as to say they should never be used. 'They can be of dubious quality, encourage spamming, and can damage the brand,' says Forbes. Instead, he wisely recommends companies to build their own opt-in lists, and that this should be a campaign objective. 'This should be seen as part of a long-term strategy to build detailed customer profiles and one-to-one interactive relationships with your customers,' he advises.

While this is good advice, it is also important to take a lateral view of mobile marketing. SMS campaigns are not just about sending out messages and waiting for a response. A two-way approach must mean just that – the messages sent from the customer are of equal importance to those sent from the company.

For customers to be involved, they must also be able to see real value. Here are some of the ways to make sure a campaign remains spam-free:

- *Gain permission.* Spam is any commercial message sent to a mobile user who has not asked to receive it. Therefore you must have the recipient's explicit permission before making contact.
- *Think laterally.* Mobile marketing does not begin and end with push campaigns. It can be integrated with other media – print, television, Internet etc – to act as a call to action, such as a text-to-enter competition.
- *Don't over-send.* A 2001 NOP survey revealed that consumers are only willing to receive around five commercial SMS marketing messages a day, wherever they are coming from.
- *Build your own database.* This not only helps you circumnavigate the spam problem, but it also means your recipients will be actively interested from the outset.
- *Be relevant.* As the Managing Director of mobile marketing firm 12 Snap, Anne de Kerckhove, observes, when targeting people via mobile devices, 'it is important to speak to them and reach them in a relevant manner'.

Spam-free services

In order to offer spam-free services, you need not only to make sure that people have opted in, but also to ensure that when they have opted out they are not contacted again. Brand2Hand, one of the companies to have pioneered the concept of 'opt in' marketing, provides a 'Text Preference Service' via the Textprefs site (www.textprefs.com). Essentially the service acts as a filter, eliminating people who have opted out of receiving commercial text messages. 'Textprefs is a free service to the industry for all comers,' explains Brand2Hand's Marketing Director, Richard Lander. 'We believe that the value of keeping spam out of SMS enhances the potential value of this business medium for everyone involved, and anything that we can do to help will be good for our business.'

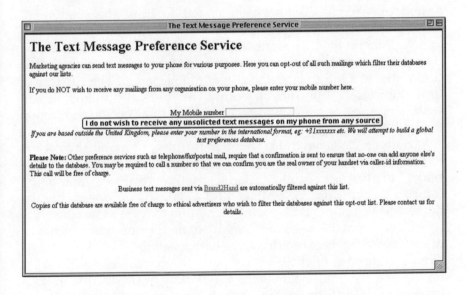

Figure 5.1   Brand2Hand's Text Preference Service eliminates opt-out consumers

Mobile marketing regulations

The growth in SMS marketing has inevitably led to some concerns. Interestingly, however, many of these concerns have been voiced by marketers themselves. Perhaps worried that overzealous marketers would jeopardize the whole future of mobile marketing (just as 'spammers' did with e-mail), various industry bodies have been busy telling marketers what is and is not good practice.

One of the first was the Wireless Advertising Association (WAA), a global organization made up of major European and US companies such as Nokia, Microsoft and CNN Internet. The WAA standards seek to clarify what exactly constitutes a wireless ad, as well as how different types of SMS ads should be classified. It has also set up similar guidelines for WAP and PDAs.

In Britain, the Mobile Marketing Association (MMA) has drawn up a code of practice intended to limit the sending of unsolicited text messages. BT Cellnet, Vodafone and Orange (among others) have all signed up to the code. The MMA has also set up a customer complaints system and a consumer protection committee in a bid to curb the rise of mobile spam. The Australian Communications Information Forum (ACIF) is also following suit with a similar set of guidelines advocating opt-in marketing models.

Various analysts have also joined in the plea for mobile marketers to adopt a responsible approach. For instance, Andrew Sergeant, a senior analyst at Jupiter Media Metrix, believes marketing campaigns delivered via SMS should have stricter 'opt-in' regulations. 'Marketers should be using standards that are more conservative than might be used for e-mail marketing or other forms of direct marketing because this form of marketing is more intrusive.' Even the European Union has got in on the act, calling for the right for people to choose whether or not they want to opt in to a marketing campaign, rather than having to make the effort to actively opt out.

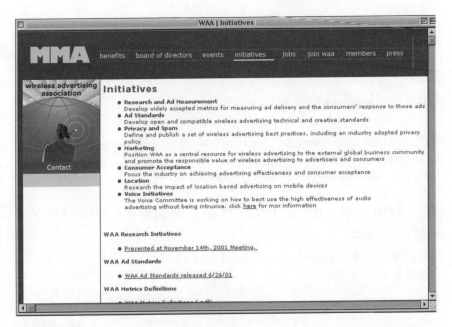

Figure 5.2 The Mobile Marketing Association is leading the global crusade against mobile spam

---

Case study: spam stuck on the menu for South African mobile users

---

In South Africa, the busiest Web site in the country is one that allows users to send SMS messages to cellphones. The MTN SMS site in fact has around 6 million registered users, which makes it one of the biggest in the world in terms of registered user base.

However, this can lead to problems when things go wrong, as in the case of a Globalnet SMS spam that went out to MTN account holders. Furthermore, the message repeatedly arrived on each user's phone owing to a technical glitch. This inevitably caused serious damage to the senders' image as marketers. The situation was made even worse by the fact that this particular message concluded with the line: 'NB: SMS replies won't be answered'. When the phone number supplied was phoned, callers were advised that it was 'impossible to personally speak to you at this stage', and taken through an automated process which at no stage revealed what service was being offered.

Spam: industry perspectives

As the following five comments attest, most mobile marketers and industry bodies now appreciate the counterproductive impact unsolicited commercial messages can have.

1.   Steve Wunker, Chairman, Mobile Marketing Association

The Mobile Marketing Association has a strict Code of Conduct that requires users to provide prior consent before receiving marketing messages. Firms that break the Code face a range of sanctions, from blacklisting to being cut off by network operators from mobile services. Consumers can also register their mobile numbers, for free, with the Direct Marketing Association's Telephone Preference Service, and firms must by law exclude those numbers from their lists. Furthermore, the EU has recently mandated that SMS be sent only with prior consent, and the government will now start moving to codify this requirement into law.

Operators are also strongly against mobile spam. They will consider a range of sanctions against abusers, including disconnecting them from their SMS Centres. They also provide their complaints to the MMA so we can co-ordinate against the worst offenders.

2.   Mark Selby, Founder, Mobile Channel Network

Spam is bad for many reasons. For the recipient, spam consumes limited SIM card and phone memory, can prevent other time-critical messages being received and is a chore to delete. Rather than promoting a product or service in a positive manner, the recipient is invariably left with an extremely negative attitude towards the brand. The frustration at not being able to stop messages being sent is intense. By contrast, permission-based mobile marketing services with clear opt-out procedures and a correct balance between promotional messages and actual content can be a pleasure to receive and a very effective marketing method.

Spam falls into two broad categories: pure marketing promotion and attempts to generate revenue immediately (through high charge SMS pull or premium priced audio lines). The former is incompetent marketing, the latter is far more serious. While SMS traffic volumes are very high today, as many as 70 per cent of post-pay mobile customers have yet to send their first SMS. When these people get an SMS telling them to call a premium priced audio line, many of them do it automatically without realizing the cost.

It is important for both consumers and marketers that procedures are implemented to prevent the growth of mobile spam, to protect consumers and to advance a very exciting form of media. Without it, the potential for mobile marketing looks bleak.

3.   Edward Orr, Vice President, UCP AG

I think spam will actually prove to be self regulating as the very essence of marketing is to attract potential customers to purchase a product or service. Annoying the hell out of a potential customer by spamming them is hardly likely to generate much business from them. Therefore I don't expect people who try annoying spamming to stay in business very long. The vast majority of credible marketers, however, will avoid spam and rather concentrate on how to take advantage of the incredible interactive power of SMS.

At UCP we have a database of approximately 2 million unique mobile numbers from subscribers to our SMS portals. However, we refuse to sell that data because we don't want our users to be spammed and we want to maintain the integrity of our products. Instead we are launching an explicitly defined opt-in database for people who actively want to receive product information and promotions via their mobile.

4.   John Farmer, Co-Founder, Carbon Partners

Mobile spam is a very important topic for all involved in the mobile services industry. After all, we're dealing with a communication channel that is uniquely personal to people. For the consumer, a mobile phone is more than just a tech gadget. It's a lifestyle device that has a major impact on our daily communication activities. Companies should respect this and consider the sensitive use of mobile marketing to deliver real benefits to the consumer. Service providers, companies and brands have an opportunity to learn from the developments within the last big communication leap, e-mail, and consider the most effective way to manage the development of the mobile marketing sector to preserve its value. Organizations such as the Mobile Marketing Association are taking the lead in establishing appropriate codes of practice.

5. Richard Lander, Marketing Director, Brand2Hand

The SMS marketing space is a pioneer environment. It is virgin territory, with no pollution and plenty of natural resources. One of the biggest threats to the value of the SMS message is spam. Spam is the lawless desperado, shredding the peace and beauty of this unspoiled place. There is a thin line, but a firm line, between welcome and unwelcome communications. We all hate intrusions into our privacy, but we all love to get a personal service. Perception is reality in this field, and we must make sure that the reality of personal service is not crowded out by the bogey of mindless interruptions.

Avoiding message fatigue

The first question any marketer should ask him or herself prior to implementing a mobile campaign is, 'Does each recipient want to receive this message?' If the target recipients have not signed up or 'opted in' to receive the message then the answer is almost always 'no'. Even if you are 100 per cent convinced that each recipient will be ecstatic to hear what you have to say, if they have not asked to hear it you should always resist.

However, even when someone has opted in to receive marketing material via SMS or any other mobile format, you should not assume that you can send out anything. If you send messages out too often or with too little thought about their usefulness, then recipients will probably be tempted to opt out from your database.

Here are some of the tried and tested ways to ensure that your send-outs are welcomed by your opt-in subscribers:

- *Send at appropriate times.* It is important to get the timing right for each send-out. Most SMS marketing send-outs are sent between 7am and 10pm in order to avoid annoying subscribers. If you are sending out messages to international mobile users then it will be necessary to take different time zones into consideration. However, there may be instances when later times are acceptable, for instance a nightclub sending out messages to regular club goers as the night is underway. The other point with regard to time is relevancy. For instance, *Top of the Pops* magazine sends out messages to its SMS subscribers on Friday evenings to coincide with the *Top of the Pops* television show.

- *Think of tangible value.* Before sending out any message, marketers need to be sure that mobile users can see tangible value. If you are only reminding them of something they already know this is unlikely.
- *Facilitate topic selection.* There is a fine line between persuasive and invasive wireless marketing. To make sure you stay on the right side of it, you could offer a selection of topics for subscribers to select. For instance, if you sell winter sports equipment it is unlikely that any one customer will be interested in everything you have to offer. However, it is likely that a snowboarder would be interested to hear when the latest snowboard has been launched and has arrived in store.
- *Make the message do something.* There are two types of marketing message: inactive and active. An inactive marketing message merely tells the subscriber about something. An active message, on the other hand, enables the subscriber to do something. The most obvious example of this is when the message acts as a voucher, which recipients produce to receive the offer. One of the most effective forms of active message is the 'on premise' promotion, whereby subscribers are alerted of an offer when they are in the relevant store or revenue. The Carlsberg World Cup SMS promotion, detailed below, provides one example of this type of campaign.
- *Personalize the message.* 'Every mobile marketing strategy that is implemented should always rely on personalization of the information, so using a permission-based model is the most important factor,' says Mark Guthrie, UK MD of mobile marketing specialist AirMedia. 'By definition, spam is a message you are not interested in, so the likelihood of converting these messages to revenue is lower than if you had taken the time to ask personal details in the first place.'

Case study: Carlsberg's World Cup campaign

Beer and football: if there was a perfect combination by which marketers could engage the psyche of the male population then that would probably be it. So the combination of free beer and a World Cup qualifying game between England and Germany, arguably the greatest footballing rivals of all time, must be marketing nirvana.

This was certainly the opinion of Carlsberg who, in conjunction with mobile marketing firm Flytxt, chose the now legendary September 2001 England–Germany game as the basis for the largest phone coupon campaign in the UK. The campaign aimed to promote Carlsberg in 40 Punch Pub Company pubs across England and to encourage football fans to interact with the Carlsberg brand while they were watching the match. The lucky campaign participants were sent M-coupons which they could then exchange for a pint of Carlsberg. The big idea, which proved successful, was to bridge the gap between the contact with potential customers through banners and posters around pubs, and the point of purchase.

On the day of the match, pubgoers were invited to send a text message to a number displayed on a promotional banner outside the participating pubs, and Flytxt was then able to capture the location of the pubgoers. The first 50 people to sign up were sent the M-coupon. Everyone else received a text message inviting them to try again at the next match (the campaign continued throughout the rest of the qualifying games through September and October).

As with many mobile marketing campaigns, this one was completely trackable. Every M-coupon carried a number that identified exactly where the customer saw the banner, and every other related action made via SMS could also be monitored. Having conducted trials previously in the year, Carlsberg were on familiar territory. 'Following the huge success of the trials in May 2001 we were very excited about embarking on a full-scale campaign across the country,' said Carlsberg-Tetley's Customer Managing Controller, Adam Young, in a statement at the time. 'The World Cup qualifying games provide the perfect focus to this campaign.'

The campaign, as with the previous trials, was also an early indication of how text messaging, and mobile marketing in general, is not just about the youth market. 'The success of the previous campaign had proved that text messaging is not just a teen phenomenon as was previously believed, as participants are largely 18–55-year-old males,' said Carsten Boers, the Vice President of Sales and Marketing at Flytxt. The campaign also coincided with an upsurge in the number of SMS users in the UK, and September 2001 was the first time the number of text messages sent in Britain each month broke through the 1 billion barrier. This was almost double the volume for the previous September.

Although the campaign might not have been quite as momentous as the 5–1 scoreline, the right choice of event at just the right time meant that both Carlsberg and Flytxt had reason to celebrate.

Figure 5.3 Carlsberg's campaign used the World Cup to generate opt-in subscribers

Pull marketing

Generally speaking, most SMS-based marketing has been push marketing. That is to say, companies and service providers have pushed information – weather reports, football results, special promotions etc – which customers have signed up for. While there is nothing inherently wrong with this type of marketing, it does have its limitations. Most significantly, it involves one-way traffic.

Pull marketing, on the other hand, enables customers to request more specific information through their mobile devices. For instance, a cinema could set up two phone numbers for people to send text messages to: one for movie times and one for movie information (such as film reviews). In this case, both the cinema and the mobile operator could benefit financially.

The obvious advantage of pull marketing is that spam is no longer even an issue. As mobile users are actively pulling information towards them, everything they receive is welcome. Furthermore, pull marketing via mobile devices assures a higher degree of relevancy than standard push campaigns. After all, even permission-based push campaigns based on selected criteria cannot guarantee that every single recipient will welcome the message, especially as some may have signed up weeks, even months, before.

With pull marketing, however, the mobile user is asking for the information there and then. Furthermore, depending on the technology deployed, users specify the information they want to receive either by dialling a specific number, typing a certain keyword or by selecting information from the wireless Web. This means the request for information coincides almost exactly with the receipt of that information.

Marketing to children

Many of the most popular mobile services – such as ringtones and logos – are targeted at children. Of course, children are always a particularly sensitive market. The fact that the services most likely to appeal to them often involve premium rates makes the situation even more worrying. While older teenagers are obviously able to make up their own minds, younger children are often misled. ICSTIS (Independent Committee for the Supervision of Standards of Telephone Information Services) is just one organization that has tried to clamp down on the problem. 'Companies that go against the children's provisions in our codes, such as charging night-rates, will face tough sanctions,' says ICSTIS spokesperson Rob Dwight. The problem is that with premium SMS services, children are often unaware of all the conditions. For any campaign aimed at the youth market the best advice is to state clearly what the service involves and, ideally, never to run premium services.

In Europe, Sweden and Greece have restraints in advertising to children, and ads that go direct to children's mobiles unmonitored by parents will cause understandable concern.

Mobile mentor: Jeremy Wright, Co-Founder, Enpocket

Note for an explosive new medium: handle with care

How should marketers take advantage of the SMS opportunity? While one answer is to move as fast as you can to capitalize on the effectiveness of a medium that is delivering response rates in the 10–30 per cent range and prompted campaign awareness levels of over 50 per cent, the other is to proceed with caution. Commercial development of this hitherto personal space needs care, which means ensuring communications are well received by your specified audience groups before more general roll out.

Below are three areas to consider: the personal nature of the medium; the potential for dialogue and the critical importance of targeting.

Personal messaging

Mobile phones are personal and people will not take kindly to having their screens cluttered with irrelevant or annoying commercial messages. So the key question to ask in planning a campaign to your target audience, is what's in it for them?

The principle that goes 'it is the few that respond that matter to prove return on investment' does not apply here. You can cause more negative reaction to your brand through targeting the wrong people with the wrong message in wireless than probably in any other medium. And there is literally no benefit to delivering repeats of the same message. Because each SMS announces its presence and demands to be viewed, the repeat will annoy and likely alienate those who may have been well disposed in the first instance.

So accurate targeting and sensitive offer/promotion development that really considers how people may react, good and not so good, is key.

Rewarding dialogue

To think of SMS as limited to 160 characters can be misleading, as wireless in fact opens up an entirely new, powerful form of marketing through involving the customer in dialogue. No other medium offers such simple and natural ability to text a response or click to call, response mechanisms that are pre-conditioned in the user through the way they already use the medium. This is quite different to direct mail, where at its best the receiver can be prompted to reach for a pen or pick up a phone. And SMS is more of a 'chat' response medium than e-mail.

Research conducted by Enpocket has shown that an enticement to enter a draw by replying 'Yes' via SMS is far more valued by the target audience if it is followed by a simple follow-up message that acknowledges receipt of the entry and states when the results of the draw will be announced. Sounds obvious, but you cannot do it so easily and instantly with other media, so it merits attention.

Similarly, interaction through SMS opens up the ability to drill down into customers' personal interests, through planning a variety of Q & A paths that build the sense that the marketer is tuned to their needs and, in reality, can take the marketer several important steps closer to a sale.

In all this, there is inclination for users to see communications as special to them, which is very powerful. And here marketers benefit from the fact that all messages, personal and commercial, are in the same text format. In this regard there are moves to ensure that all commercial messages received are identified as such. But this does not take away the fact that consumers are particularly receptive and responsive to communications containing an offer or proposition that they see as exclusive to them via SMS and not generally available through other means.

Targeting

Wireless targeting can be truly remarkable. No other medium has media owners with such a broad and potent range of targeting criteria for maximizing relevance and minimizing waste. The mobile operators hold all the keys: demographics, location (home and roaming), phone usage, phone types and reach (all mobile users). And they have the customer relationships, so it is in their best interests to ensure that the audience you seek to reach appreciates the campaign or they could face damaging customer churn.

However, beware less scrupulous list brokers. There are a number of companies developing opt-in lists through offers of free content, such as ringtones, graphics or alert services. While these lists will offer some demographic targeting, there is no onus on the list provider to control the frequency, type or volume of messages the customer receives and they generally have no ability to control duplication with other opt-in lists. In time it is hoped that clear opt-out policies will be consistently deployed and understood by consumers. In the main, however, it is advisable to buy media from owners who have ultimate responsibility for their customer base.

And when it comes to assessing customer reaction, there is no better medium. Wireless media literally is the numbers that can be called to gauge consumer reaction through a telephone questionnaire. So messages that incur no production costs, can be simply and cheaply tested, refined and rolled out against specific audiences.

Results

There is much yet to be learnt, and the overriding finding of all the research studies Enpocket has conducted point to the need for marketers to develop more relevant and creative campaigns. Yet, however critical consumers may be, SMS is currently driving phenomenal response rates, many times higher than those achieved by the Web in its early days. And this with a cost per message that is a fraction of typical mail shot costs.

In such a medium, where production costs are negligible, there is therefore much to be gained by putting significant effort and resource into the tightest targeting of propositions, offers and tone of voice to deliver the best results from specific audience groups.

Jeremy Wright is Co-Founder of Enpocket, the first UK wireless media sales house.

Text overload

As mobile marketing increases in popularity, the potential for 'text overload' becomes a worry for both users and marketers. If mobile users become swamped by marketing messages, the danger is that permission-based messages will be just as unwelcome as mobile spam.

Location-based services, whereby shops and services target nearby consumers, could end up being particularly annoying for mobile users walking down a busy high street. When these and other forms of commercial message are counted on top of a potential increase in personal messaging, saturation point may not be too far away.

While there is not much each individual marketer can do about the overall situation, aside from support organizations such as the MMA, it is important to bear the problem of overload in mind. When sending out marketing messages it is all too easy to forget the context within which they are received. Although a message may be the first of your campaign, it is un- likely that it will be the first message of the day arriving on the recipient's mobile. In other words, no campaign exists in a vacuum; every message sent out arrives into an increasingly crowded environment. To justify their activity, marketers must not be seen to contribute to the problem. Over-sending messages, however worthwhile their content may be, will only prove counterproductive.

Legal implications

Responsible marketing means taking into account the legal regulations. Many countries, particularly those in the European Union, have strict laws regarding direct marketing. Some countries have specific restrictions on certain forms of advertising. Germany, for instance, has various laws regarding promotional campaigns via the Internet, and these restrictions are also likely to be upheld against text message campaigns.

In the UK, there are two pieces of legislation to consider. Firstly, there is the Data Protection Act 1998 which protects consumers against unsolicited e-mails and, by implication, unsolicited text messages. This law gives individuals the right to sue as well as the possibility of action from the Information Commissioner.

The other relevant legislation is the catchily titled Telecommunications (Data Protection and Privacy) Regulations 1999. As with the 1998 Act, no specific reference is made to text messaging, principally because marketing via SMS was yet to take off when the regulations were drawn up. However, as this legislation was designed to stamp out other intrusive forms of marketing (such as fax-outs and cold calls), the implications for SMS spammers are clear.

Last word

Various consumer, industry and governmental organizations around the world have voiced their concerns regarding irresponsible and unethical mobile marketing. The ultimate deterrent, however, is that this type of marketing simply does not work. The only impact companies can make by sending out unrequested, indiscriminate or irrelevant messages is a negative one. The real rewards of mobile marketing can only be reaped by focusing on what potential and actual customers want to receive, as opposed to just thinking what the marketer wants to achieve. It may sound obvious, but it is a lesson some companies have yet to learn.

six

Generation text

The importance of the youth market has long been recognized by companies looking to establish lifelong customers or generate a brand image. In terms of mobile marketing, however, this market has a further significance. This is because it has been the younger sectors of the population who have pioneered the use of new mobile technologies, particularly those based around text messaging. Therefore, even those companies and organizations that do not directly target the youth market can benefit from taking a closer look at their messaging habits. The purpose of this chapter is to provide that 'closer look'.

The new power generation

In the late 1980s and 1990s a stereotypical image of a Western teenager would have been that of a spotty kid in a Nirvana T-shirt sat spaced out in front of MTV with a finger on the remote control. Nowadays, of course, the image would be pretty much the same, only instead of flicking channels, the teenager would probably be punching at text messages on his or her mobile (and the T-shirt would probably say 'Limp Bizkit'). From Beavis and Butthead to Beavis and TextHead in ten years – well, that's progress for you.

Actually, that really is progress, at least it is from the perspective of the youth marketer. Instead of spending millions on hard-to-monitor television advertising campaigns, marketers can now target audiences much more cost-effectively and with greater precision via mobile devices. Anyway, progress or not, the fact that the use of text messaging, along with most other present day applications, was pioneered by teenagers is widely recognized. An understanding of how and why teens and young adults use their mobile devices is therefore useful for any marketer looking to exploit this medium.

Indeed, in an article I wrote for the *Guardian* newspaper in October 2001, entitled 'Teenage clicks', I noted the ways in which teen technologies such as SMS and Instant Messenger eventually become mainstream. While I stand by this view, it is important to realize that when it comes to mobile technology, teenagers are already the mainstream, at least if the mainstream can be measured in numbers alone. Unlike other teen phenomena, mobile phones do not divide youth audiences: everyone either wants one or already has one. For teenagers in Europe and Asia, mobile phones are no longer a luxury or an accessory, they are a badge of existence.

This chapter will start by taking a look at some of the factors that have contributed to the popularity of mobile devices among this all-important age group.

Teen text

Across the globe, by far the most active group of text fanatics are teenagers, who have rapidly made SMS their favourite means of communication. According to Anne de Kerckhove, Managing Director of mobile marketing agency 12Snap, SMS provides the perfect means of reaching a young audience. 'Mobile is the primary mode of communication for teenagers,' she reminds us. 'Sixteen-to-eighteen-year-olds text message on average eight times a day – that's more than e-mail or voice calls. They see mobiles as an integral part of their social life, an extension of their personality and social circles.'

The fact that SMS has proved especially popular among teen users is hardly a surprise, say some mobile experts. Not only does active mobile communication act as a signifier of a healthy social life, as 12Snap's de Kerckhove has observed, but it also provides that most desired teenage attribute – independence. 'The mobile phone presents the teenage market with a distinct opportunity to take control of their own communications, free from the previous limitations of the home phone or computer which were more closely monitored by parents,' says John Farmer, Co-Founder of SMS application and service provider Carbon Partners. The strong bond teens develop with their mobile is also evidenced by the ways in which they personalize their phone (via ringtones, logos, multi-coloured phone covers and so on).

The reason text messaging has overtaken voice calls in popularity is equally apparent. (According to a Carbon Partners survey, text messaging is favoured because it is cheaper than making a voice call, it is considered more convenient and also seen as a cooler way to communicate – see below.) Most significantly of all, at least from the marketer's perspective, teens have so far proved very responsive to SMS-based marketing campaigns. As Steve Wunker, Chairman and Founder of the Wireless Marketing Association, has observed, 'Mobile is just about the most targeted form of mass market advertising imaginable'.

According to PWS's Chief Executive, Anthony Stonefield, the key lies in making sure mobile users perceive immediate value from an opt-in exchange. He also believes it is important to acknowledge the 'cool factor' of text messaging: 'Our goal is to keep things cool. Mobile is all about a cool entertainment environment.'

Explaining the teen text phenomenon

Research by Carbon Partners, a company which provides SMS text messaging applications and services, on the mobile phone and text messaging habits of over 500 young British adults, identified that texting is popular among teens for three main reasons. These are:

● *Cost*. The fact that sending a text message is cheaper than making a voice call is one clear incentive.
● *Convenience*. Although there are disputes regarding the usability of SMS, many believe that it is more convenient than sending an e-mail or making a voice call.
● *The cool factor*. While text messaging remains associated with youth, it also inevitably becomes viewed as cool. As use continues to grow among older users, the less cool it will become.

According to Carbon Partners' Co-Founder John Farmer (who contributes to this chapter), the teenage market was the first to work around the interface limitations involved in text messaging. 'There was no perceived obstacle in the fact that it takes three clicks to get a letter, and as such we've seen text messaging grow fastest first in the teenage market before moving into other demographics.' The problem is that although the three Cs (cost, convenience and cool) may go some way in explaining why texting became the new favourite pastime among European teens, it does not fully account for how it became successful. The success of SMS has certainly caused some head scratching for the proponents of usability.

After all, the golden rule of usability – which states that success depends on how easy the medium is to use – does not seem to apply to SMS. Not only are the problems of tiny screens and keypads obvious, but there is also the fact that SMS came after mobile phones. That is to say, mobile phones have been designed primarily for voice calls, not SMS. As such, keypads are arranged around numbers, not the alphabet.

Jakob Nielsen, the ex-programmer for Sun Microsystems and the person most associated with the concept of usability, has been particularly interested in the relentless advance of SMS and the 'lousy telephone pads' used to type and send text messages. As the average amount of text messages sent per customer per month grew from 0.4 per cent in 1995 to 35 per cent by the end of 2000, the usability disciples have had to reassess their theories. 'All the wireless experts in the world never seemed to realize people's endless capacity to flirt with their current love interest and slag off their mates in 160 characters or less,' says NUA Survey's Editor Kathy Foley.

Indeed, Nielsen has been forced to broaden the principle of usability owing to the success of SMS. 'I usually promote usability,' he told subscribers of his AlertBox newsletter. 'But if truth be told, a better model is to analyse the usefulness of a service which is a combination of two parameters: utility (what the service does; how closely it matches users' needs) and usability.' He then went on to say that, although he has doubts regarding the usability of SMS, it has 'very high utility'. He even suggests that the high utility is a consequence of poor usability – 'the messages are short and fast to read because they have to be composed on a lousy telephone keypad'.

Mobile mentor: John Farmer, Co-Founder, Carbon Partners

Teenagers define mobile messaging

It's the hottest communication medium available at the start of the 21st century. It's given birth to a new language for friends, lovers, advertisers and poets. Generating valuable millions in revenue and spawning new industries. Designed by the telecom networks? No. Text messaging has been created, defined and popularized by the teenage generation.

Teenagers have transformed our daily communication structure with their early acceptance and adoption of text messaging. Witness the speed with which people check to see where their latest text message has come from. Even mid-conversation, attention will be quickly diverted for a 15 second 'text hit'. This change in communication habits was initiated by the willingness of a teenage audience to work with and around any apparent technology limitations. This is a state of mind not to accept the limits as being defined by the technology but to take the technology and work with it. And the result? The rising interest and backing of the telecom networks in text messaging and the rapid emergence of a new communication medium throughout all demographics.

As the rest of society and the commercial world plays catch up with the teenage texters, they would be well advised to keep a close eye on the mobile messaging habits being formed in the teen generation. These are the guidelines for future opportunities.

Mobile communities are emerging whose members have shared thoughts, interests and passions. Within these communities members establish rapid and fleeting mobile-based relationships. Information, comment and recommendations are exchanged by text, taking advantage of the medium's speed, and permanent availability. Communication habits are evolving within these mobile environments. The networks, handset manufacturers and application providers are supplying the raw material and it's the teenagers who are in control of the future of mobile messaging.

Carbon Partners work with media owners, telecom networks, sports companies and FMCG brands to maximize the commercial opportunities that SMS text messaging provides; providing SMS text messaging applications and services that enable effective wireless SMS marketing and open new revenue generating opportunities.

Mobile culture

For the younger members of European and Asian society, mobile devices are about more than technology – they represent an entire culture. More accurately, they represent an updated version of youth culture that is defined via this still relatively new mode of social interaction.

Unlike other technocultures, such as those associated with desktop computing or home automation, the mobile culture is something people are proud to belong to. As mobile culture is about much more than technology, there is no obvious geek factor. In fact, in many parts of the developed world, it has now become more embarrassing for teenagers not to be a part of this culture. Text messaging is now one of the chief ways in which some people communicate. To be without an SMS compatible mobile device therefore means being outside certain social circles, and for teens and young adults this can be devastating.

So it is easy to see how mobile culture became so cool, so quickly. It is also no coincidence that the first companies to exploit the potential for mobile marketing were streetwise, youth-focused brands such as those nightclubs in Ibiza that decided to send clubbers their DJ line-ups via SMS in the summer of 2000.

As mobile culture has grown, its cool status has been confirmed and reconfirmed by its inclusion within relevant media. The UK's leading music weekly, the *NME*, has included a mobile ringtone chart since the beginning of 2001. Leading club culture magazines such as *Mixmag*, *Ministry* and *Muzik* have also run a variety of articles, features and promotions based around mobile devices.

There are even youth lifestyle magazines now dedicated entirely to the 'mobile generation'. The print magazine and Web site *Monster Mob* (www.monstermob.com), abbreviated simply as *Mob*, was the first such title to hit UK news-stands. Although there had been technology and industry-oriented mobile magazines (such as *Mobile News*, *Mobile Communications International* and *Mobile User*), this was the first magazine to present mobile usage as a lifestyle choice. Early issues of this lateral-minded magazine placed articles on mobile communications alongside articles which have no direct relation to mobile devices but which were likely to interest young(ish) mobile users. Therefore one issue included features on celebrities such as Kelis and Dr Dre alongside in-depth features on the history of prank calls and flirting via mobile devices. (However, each celebrity article kept to the mobile theme by including relevant ringtone and logo numbers.)

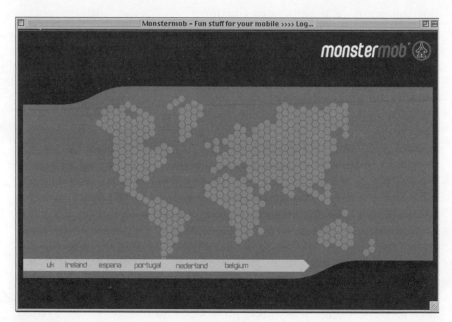

Figure 6.1   Monster Mob: presenting mobile usage as a lifestyle choice

It is not just magazines, either. Television shows have also got in on the act: MTV has even got its own text request show. The lesson youth marketers are still learning is that mobile culture extends beyond mobile technology. It is slowly but surely having an influence on the whole of youth culture itself, from music and movies to television and magazines.

Pay-as-you-go

One of the main factors that contributed to the popularity of mobile devices among teenagers, if not the main factor, was the arrival of pay-as-you-go phones. Before the existence of pay-as-you-go, parents were understandably concerned about their teenage offspring using a mobile phone. Parental nightmares of astronomical bills certainly prevented many teens from going mobile. When the pay-as-you-go system arrived in the late 1990s, parents' fears were alleviated. Now mums and dads were provided with some form of credit control, and limits could be placed on usage.

This also helps to explain the phenomenal rise of teenage SMS text messaging which occurred in many places, particularly in Europe, towards the end of the last decade. With their use of mobile devices effectively metered, teens turned to a communications medium that was not only fun, but also inexpensive.

Customizable mobiles

Shortly after pay-as-you-go devices started to take off, the mobile manufacturers hit upon another great marketing concept: the clip-on cover. Although they are often warranted little more than a footnote in the history of the mobile revolution, the importance of customizable covers for mobile devices – at least among the teenage market – is considerable.

Figure 6.2   Customizable mobiles are helping turn mobiles into individual devices

By being able to personalize their mobile device in this way, teens are turning mobiles into individual devices and strengthening the mobile/user bond. In Europe, Nokia has been particularly sharp in spotting the potential for different, detachable phone covers. By Christmas 2001, the company had made detachable covers available for its lower priced models such as the Nokia 3310, the 3330 and even more expensive models such as the 8210.

The covers included Stars and Stripes, Union Jacks, polka dots, fluorescent colours, animal prints, snakeskin, leopard skin, zebra, Dalmatian, and a various assortment of other aesthetically unsettling designs. Although not to everyone's taste, clip-on covers are an unqualified success in the youth market and are a key driver in the purchasing of mobile devices. Their popularity indicates how young people view their devices – as a signifier of their individuality certainly, but also as a source of fun. The fact that national flags, football club logos and pop stars are among the most sought after designs also supports the 'tribal' element of mobile use, particularly of text messaging, which many commentators have identified.

Case study: Cadbury 'goes large'

Cadbury launched the biggest-ever text message promotion on 10 of its chocolate bar brands in 2001.

The promotion, which was undertaken by wireless marketing company Flytxt and ran on 65 million chocolate bars, was integrated with a related TV ad campaign. Reference to the campaign appeared on wrappers and alerted consumers to a phone number and a unique code inside the wrapper which they sent as an SMS message to find out if they had won a prize. The chocolate bars, which included Crunchie, Caramel and Dairy Milk, all carried the promotion for two months during the summer.

The campaign proved so successful that even Willy Wonka would have been proud. Hundreds of thousands of chocoholics from across the UK participated, partly because it was so widely advertised. However, not only was the promotion heavily advertised, but consumers were offered very strong incentives. Prizes worth more than £1 million included £5,000 cash giveaways, DVD players and Sony PlayStation consoles. These prizes were therefore relevant to this predominantly youth-focused campaign.

'This is the biggest text message campaign in terms of the reach of products and of consumers,' said Flytxt's Chief Executive Lars Becker at the time. A Cadbury spokesman said: 'This is our first venture in the wireless sector and we're tapping into a huge market. We chose to run it on single chocolate bars that are generally impulse purchases by the young.' Cadbury said at the time they would use entrants' mobile phone numbers to target any future onpack promotion, but as yet there are no plans to use the numbers for any other marketing purpose.

Ringtones

Not content with making their phone simply look unique, many people choose to make them sound different too. By choosing a musical ringtone that expresses their personality (or, even better, by composing their own ringtone), mobile users are able to individualize their mobile devices even further.

Whether it is the latest number one or the *1812 Overture*, mobile ringtones are big business, and particularly popular with teens. Following the success the i-Mode system first experienced in Japan, downloadable ringtones are now a hit well beyond Asia, especially in Europe. As an indication of this popularity, one of the UK's leading music magazines, the *NME*, publishes a weekly ringtones chart alongside standard singles and album charts. Again, it was Nokia who had its finger on the teenage pulse and who acted the fastest of all Western mobile companies in acknowledging the market potential for downloadable ringtones. However, nowadays most manufacturers ensure their devices make it possible for users to download any ringtone they choose.

According to Bill Sunner, the Managing Director for Irish ringtone company Dialaring.com, ringtones appeal to people because 'everybody likes to put their own individual touch to whatever it is they have'. As many phones now have more than one ringtone, they can reflect people's moods. They can even have different ringtones to let you know a certain person is calling.

The popularity of non-standard ringtones, along with individualized covers, may at first seem like a side issue for mobile marketers.

However, this popularity indicates just how far form has surpassed function in relation to mobile phones. Or, more accurately, how far the function itself has changed. Just as a car is no longer simply a way of getting from A to B, it is equally true that a mobile phone is no longer just a convenient aid to communication. An individualized mobile ringtone, like the mobile phone itself, acts as a social signifier – enabling young users to simultaneously be a part of, and apart from, the social circle. For teens, as well as many older mobile phone owners, the phone represents a communications device and status symbol rolled into one. A ringtone can therefore act in several different ways – as a call alert, as a way of indicating what music you are into, as a way of expressing a sense of humour, even as a technological mating call.

As well as ringtones and clip-on covers, downloadable logos such as those of pop groups, football teams and images of cartoons have enabled people to customize their phones even further.

Figure 6.3 Downloadable ringtones and logos are increasingly popular among teen markets

Mobile gaming

The rapidly growing popularity of mobile gaming provides another indication that the mobile phone – at least for the youth market – is now used for more than just communication. Furthermore, the large mobile companies were quick to recognize this fact. For instance, in July 2001 the Vice President and General Manager of Core Solutions for Motorola's Internet Software and Content Group announced that, 'Motorola strongly believes that the games and entertainment environment is key to the development of mainstream success in GPRS and 3G, for operators, manufacturers and developers'.

At around the same time, Nokia increased phone-user options by offering games that could be downloaded via various Nokia sites, such as their UK Club Nokia site (club.nokia.co.uk). In 2002, as I write this book, these games are getting more advanced, with Siemens and Motorola as well as Nokia producing more sophisticated downloadable games.

So far, some interesting trends have emerged. Mobile game developers such as Digital Bridges and iFone have taken mobile users back to the early 1980s, having developed mobile versions of old arcade classics such as Space Invaders, Asteroids, Galaxian and Frogger.

Figure 6.4   IFone's Frogger is taking mobile users back to the 1980s

However, while these developers looked back to the past for game inspiration, they – along with many others in the mobile industry – looked forward to the new Java-enabled devices which these games were designed for. Indeed, Java – the technology that makes dynamic graphics a possibility for mobile devices – is already revolutionizing the whole mobile market. Nokia for one expects to put the technology into 100 million mobile phones by the end of 2003. Siemens and Motorola have also launched a variety of Java-based devices. By putting processing power into Java-enabled handsets, such as the Motorola Accompli or the Siemens SL45I, they have not only provided better animation, but also the ability to download new games at any time.

'Java offers for the first time real cross-platform opportunities,' says Annika Faeshe, Siemens' Marketing Manager for smart devices. 'Loaded once either via PC or "over the air" and locally stored on the phone, users can play Java games anywhere and anytime without network connection. Even sophisticated multiplayer games with network connection are possible.'

Java has also benefited from the experience of WAP. 'There's been a lot of important lessons learnt from WAP, especially with announcing a system that's hard for the consumer to grasp, with very misleading ad campaigns and no content,' says Matt Spall, the managing director of mobile games developer, Morpheme.

One of the reasons why there was such early confidence in mobile gaming was that it had taken off elsewhere, most notably in Japan. There, NTT DoCoMo's i-Mode managed to turn mobile gaming into a viable business with millions of Japanese teens and young adults playing mobile games. By 2001, over 10 per cent of transactions on I-Mode game, Bandai's Meru De Koishite ('Love via e-mail' – a game in which players have to send text messages to one of seven virtual lovers) had been played by around half a million people. By 2005, the research company Jupiter Media Metrix predicts that mobile gaming in Japan should be generating $2.5 billion in paid content.

'The huge success of i-Mode in Japan, where two-thirds of use is for entertainment, shows the potential that can be achieved elsewhere,' explains Rob Gear, an analyst at the analyst and consulting company Ovum.

Datamonitor predicted the worldwide mobile gaming market to be worth nearly $17 billion in 2006. However, others are striking a more cautious note. Ovum, for instance, place the figure at $6 billion and have stated that 'consumers will be willing to pay only where they perceive value'. This view is supported by Jupiter analyst Billy Pigeon, who reckons that 'not everything that has worked in Japan will develop well here. The differences are not just cultural, but technological, and – with DoCoMo having a 70 per cent market share – a difference in the business structure.'

That fact acknowledged, the signs so far seem to be good and most of the main developers, operators and manufacturers feel confident that mobile gaming will eventually extend beyond the youth market. Furthermore, as it offers far more opportunities than either its WAP or SMS equivalents, Java is seen as the way forward. According to industry insiders, SMS has only really proved workable for text-based adventures and quizzes, and WAP has lacked animation and left users waiting for command responses. In contrast, they say that Java offers greater usability. The use of GPRS (general packet radio service) alongside Java also means that download times are a lot faster. Java-enabled devices should ultimately lead to greater customer satisfaction as users just have to click on games, download the one they want and play it.

However, whether or not the mobile gaming evangelists keep singing from the same (Java-enabled) hymn sheet remains to be seen. Despite the Java hype, SMS should not be written off. After all, some of the most successful mobile games to date, widely adopted by teens and older mobile users, are SMS-based games such as Who Wants to be a Millionaire.

Furthermore, the significance of mobile gaming should not be underestimated by those without a direct stake in the games industry. Indeed, many mobile marketing campaigns, such as that for the 2001 blockbuster *Planet of the Apes*, include a gaming element. Moreover, while teens remain the chief mobile pioneers, mobile games provide them with one of the greatest incentives to try something new. For instance, the first colour games provided a chief incentive for mobile users to purchase the first European mobile with a colour screen, the Ericsson T68. In turn, colour screens are increasing youth interest in multimedia messaging, a way of attaching colour documents (still pictures in video and audio clips) to text messages. Therefore, by keeping an eye on the future of mobile gaming, marketers can also get a clearer picture of mobile usage in general.

The text epidemic

In many parts of Europe the number of young people sending text messages outweighs the number making voicecalls or sending e-mails. Indeed, such is the popularity of text messaging among teens, it has even brought with it its own epidemic – TMI, or text message injury. This refers to the painful swelling and inflammation of mobile users' fingers and thumbs from sending too many text messages. Andrew Chadwick, director of the British RSI (Repetitive Strain Injuries) Association told the *Mirror* newspaper that the phenomenal popularity of text messaging causes a whole new batch of problems. 'We're talking about people making hundreds of tiny repeated movements as they use the mobile keypad,' he explained. 'Because the movements are small they do not cause the blood to circulate, and that means the fingers are acting like an engine without oil.' He also stated that children in particular are prone to TMI.

While the health hazards may be real, Chadwick's concerns are counterbalanced by others who believe text messaging may actually be good for our health. They argue that, though repetitive strain is a risk, it is not as serious as the damage from radiation risked when making voice calls. In this scenario text messaging becomes the lesser of two evils.

It is worth pointing out that every time a new communications medium has taken off – be it the telephone, the television or even the Internet – health issues have been raised, particularly the way in which they impact on children. Moreover, any medical concerns seem unlikely to deter the tide of texters. According to 'SMS poet' Andy Wilson, most mobile users adopt the ostrich position when it comes to techno health scares. 'The whole of Britain may well sue the phone manufacturers in 20 years' time for our arthritic thumbs, but in the meantime we're enjoying this cute new way of communicating with each other.'

Ten teen commandments

Although text message marketing to teens can bring immense

rewards, it is easier to get wrong than any other area of mobile marketing. So while defining the key to a successful youth campaign may be as worthwhile as guessing the length of a piece of string, there are some general principles that can be adopted. As the following ten commandments attest, youth-focused wireless campaigns should be handled very carefully indeed:

1. *Think context.* Make sure messages fit within a relevant context. If a recipient asks 'Why have I been sent this message?' the battle is already lost.
2. *Be cool.* According to Premium Wireless Service's Chief Executive Anthony Stonefield, it is important to acknowledge the cool factor of text messaging. 'Our goal is to keep things cool,' he says. 'Mobile is all about a cool entertainment environment.' However, overplaying the cool card may have counterproductive results, leading to what some youth marketers refer to as DDS – Disco Dad Syndrome.
3. *Know when to keep quiet.* As Carbon Partners' John Farmer observes, 'the mobile is a distinctly personal device and care must be taken to respect this factor when targeting teenagers. Intrusive, or over marketed, messages will potentially do more damage than good.'
4. *Don't send spam.* Although some research has suggested that teen mobile users often welcome unsolicited SMS messages, there is a growing fear that the rise in unwanted commercial text messages could jeopardize the whole future of mobile marketing. As Mark Mulhern, Executive Director of wireless marketing agency Rtn2Sndr, observes 'the excitement of receiving unsolicited SMS is wearing off fast'.
5. *Have a cross-media approach.* Mobile marketers have discovered that SMS-based campaigns work well in conjunction with other forms of media, such as television, radio, print and outdoor advertising. For instance, in a campaign they conducted for Channel 5, marketing agency Flytxt found that 90 per cent of viewers who responded to a television advert inviting them to send text messages to enter a competition, sent a message within 15 minutes of the advert finishing. Another successful youth-oriented campaign, Pepsi's 'Text 2 the Max' campaign worked by promoting the SMS activity on the products (Pepsi Max bottles) themselves.
6. *Make it two-way.* If a mobile campaign involves an active text

response from the target mobile user it is likely to be more effective than a one-way approach. While response rates to mobile marketing campaigns vary widely – from 4 per cent to 40 per cent according to 12Snap – SMS brand recall tends to be over 50 per cent. As the mobile phone is a mass medium with a direct response capability built in, responses tend to be rapid (12Snap claim that 70 per cent of respondents do so within 24 hours). Such direct and immediate interaction can clearly help to generate increased brand loyalty. If the mobile user sends the first message, in response to a magazine promotion for instance, the effectiveness will be increased further.

7. *Make it viral.* The fact that mobile devices are essentially peer-to-peer communication tools provides yet another advantage, and means the possibilities for viral marketing are almost limitless. The SMS campaigns that work have managed to do so by providing a genuine incentive that will encourage teens to spread the word among their peers. As Seth Godin has successfully shown in his book, *Unleashing the Idea Virus*, any marketing message which is sent from a friend is going to be at least twice as effective as those sent directly from the company itself.

8. *Build a database.* One aim of any youth mobile marketing campaign should be to lay the seeds for future correspondence. By encouraging mobile users to initiate or respond to permission-based SMS activity, it is possible to build a relevant database of keen recipients.

9. *Provide added value.* According to mobile marketing firms PWS and 12Snap, to name but two, the key lies in making sure immediate and added value is provided from an opt-in exchange.

10. *Be responsible.* Obviously this rule applies to any mobile marketing campaign. However, when marketing to under-18s via such personal devices, you could be judged not only on how valuable the information is that you are providing but also how responsibly you send it. Organizations such as the Association of Teachers and Lecturers (ATL) in the UK are watching very carefully how marketers choose to use and abuse the mobile medium. Most of all, responsibility is a matter of common sense. For instance, just because many children are interested in the occult (over 50 per cent according to one MORI poll), clearly doesn't mean marketers should feed this interest.

Case study: East West Records wireless marketing campaign for Oxide & Neutrino by Aerodean

Communicating with record-buying teenagers is notoriously difficult, particularly with fans of the more groundbreaking acts. They shun conventional media and their lifestyle makes customer contact difficult. In October 2000 the UK's first 'text fan club' was launched by East West Records, a subsidiary of Warner Records, for Oxide & Neutrino. Oxide & Neutrino is an underground UK garage act with a strong teen fanbase, so text messaging was judged to be an ideal medium. East West Records chose Aerodeon to implement the campaign.

The campaign objectives were threefold: to build a database of Oxide & Neutrino fans, to grow the database through viral marketing, and finally to associate Oxide & Neutrino with text messaging as a cool, underground medium. Flyers and postcards were distributed, inviting fans to text register by sending a text message that included date of birth, postcode and first name. In reply, each fan received personalized updates from the duo.

Building on the success of the activity, 100,000 CD inserts were printed for the duo's December single *No Good 4 Me*, with details of the text registration. This was the first on-pack text promotion in the UK. Fans were able to request logos and ringtones, via text or the Web, which had an original twist. Logos were available for Oxide, Neutrino or Oxide & Neutrino, and Neutrino created a special ringtone specifically for the campaign, which was the UK's first artist created ringtone. Within days, the size of the text fan club exceeded most fan clubs built through traditional media.

The campaign continued for the next single, *Up Middle Finger*, with a video/text tie in. As part of the *Up Middle Finger* campaign a viral mechanic was introduced via text that encouraged fans to build the biggest 'crew'. Each fan was asked to include in their text response the name of their crew, with the prize for the biggest crew being to have Oxide & Neutrino play in the winner's lounge. More than 500 crews registered and the winning crew had 59 members. Two out of every three responses were from 'new' names not previously on the database. What is most interesting about the campaign is how the SMS element was integrated at every level: even the television advert featured Oxide & Neutrino sending text messages about the new album. The album Execute was released on 28 May 2001, entering the UK charts ahead of expectations at number 11.

The campaign results were as follows:

● *Database growth*. The Oxide & Neutrino database far exceeded expectations. In October 2001 it had 30,000 names, which is a six-fold increase over the target.
● *Reduced cost*. The cost of building the database was significantly less than the cost of building a similar database through conventional media.
● *Direct interaction*. The crew viral mechanic for Oxide & Neutrino successfully attracted many new fans. Two out of three responses were 'new' names.
● *Viral success*. 'A significant driver of the sustained sales pattern for Oxide & Neutrino has been the inclusive, viral wireless marketing which encourages the fans to interact directly,' says Aerodeon's Andrew Jones.

Last word

For those marketers willing to act responsively, the advice is clear: text messaging provides the best means of reaching the teen market. Furthermore, as SMS and other text-based technologies become increasingly popular with older mobile users, there are now opportunities to reach a wider audience. Ultimately, however, the future of mobile youth marketing depends not only on how many companies get the message, but how responsively they act upon it.

seven

The language of text

The success of any marketing campaign depends on the ability to communicate with an audience in a relevant manner, and language is often a key part of this. Indeed, some advertising campaigns have been centred around one single, crucial word (think of the 1999–2000 Budweiser 'Whassup?' campaign, for instance). When it comes to text messaging, however, language is often all there is and so every word counts. This chapter looks at some of the unique factors to consider when wording a text message campaign.

A new language

One thing any marketer interested in reaching the mobile population should realize is that wireless applications have not only rewritten the marketing rulebook, but they have done so in a completely different language. The inherent limitations of mobile technology, particularly SMS which only enables you to send messages of up to 160 characters, means that marketers are having to communicate in an altogether new way. As Co-Founder of marketing firm i-level, Andrew Walmsey, has remarked, 'It's like writing a haiku, but not quite as elegant'.

George Orwell may have suggested that we should always use the short word in favour of the long, but mobile marketing requires us to favour the abbreviation over the word. To understand just how radically SMS texting can impact on language, it is worth looking at one of the short-listed entries from the *Guardian's* text message poetry competition:

> 14: /a txt msg pom./his is r bunsn brnr bl%/his hair lyk fe filings/W/ac/dc going thru./I sit by him in kemistry,/it splits my @oms/wen he :-)s @ me.

Confused? Here's the translation of Julia Bird's poem:

> 14:/a text message poem/ his eyes are bunsen burner blue,/his hair like iron filings/with ac/dc going through./I sit by him in chemistry,/it splits my atoms/when he smiles at me.

(For another example from this competition go to the case study at the end of this chapter.) Although it is unlikely, and inadvisable, that you will be using abbreviations and spelling manipulations as extreme as those used above, it is important to understand the way sentences are abbreviated.

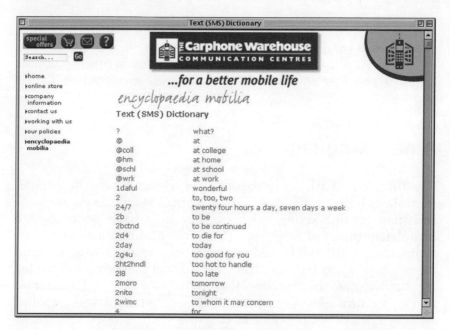

Figure 7.1   The Carphonewarehouse site translates textspeak

Indeed, as the proliferation of SMS text message dictionaries shows, keeping up with this constantly evolving lingo is big business. Acronyms such as VBG (very big grin) and WSLS (win some, lose some) are being understood by a growing number of mobile users, particularly those at the younger end of the market. Other shortcuts commonly used are emoticons, or smileys, such as :-) indicating a smiley face or ;-) signifying a wink. Phrases like 'Txt is gr8' (text is great), 'CUL8r' (see you later) and 'RU OK 4 2Nite?' also indicate how SMS users have got around the 160 character limit.

The right balance

Marketers need to realize that not everyone who sends text messages will understand the truncated language SMS has spawned. Marketers therefore need to appreciate the delicate balance between making sure the message fits the medium, and making sure the recipient of the message understands what it means. In other words, marketers shouldn't go over the top (or OTT, as we are talking text). A message that is filled with obscure and difficult abbreviations, such as '1dRfl' (meaning wonderful), is going to baffle all but the most fluent of texters.

That said, if a marketer can convey a deep understanding of the medium within the message itself, it is likely to make a positive impact. This is especially true for brands and companies with their eye on young and hip consumers. Indeed, some believe that the offshoot of the English language text has created – where letters, numbers and emoticons can fit together in the same phrase or sentence – is used by teens as a form of self-identification. This is certainly the view of Brian Sheridan, Head of Product Development at Eircell, an Irish mobile phone operator. 'I personally believe that text is the new language of youth culture, a graffiti, if you like,' he told *Wired* magazine. 'And some of these messages can really take a while to decipher, it's like a code among teenagers.'

Text misconceptions

With some young users sending in excess of 250 messages a month, it is perhaps unsurprising that text has bred its own language. However, some believe that, even with regard to the youth market, the language is not completely new. 'There is a general misconception that the guides to SMS shorthand which are available everywhere actually indicate the way people really communicate via SMS,' says Andrew Jones, Managing Director of the award-winning UK mobile marketing agency, Aerodeon. 'In fact, even teenagers rarely communicate in acronyms.'

Jones does, however, acknowledge that SMS is a medium which does encourage a certain inventiveness of language, and he expresses the necessity for marketers to communicate in a relevant way to their market without going too far. 'As far as the language is concerned, we carry out regular analysis based on the thousands of messages we receive each day across a large range of magazines and demographics so that when we send messages to people it is in their own "language",' he said. Therefore, by analysing real text messages that teens are sending to each other and to magazines, Aerodeon is able to get inside the minds, or at least the mobiles, of the most text-friendly population segment.

Here is a cross-section of text messages received for a recent issue of teen girl magazine, J17, which is one of the magazines Aerodeon has run a service for (some of these were printed in the magazine):

Example 1:
i am going 2 a disco 2moro nite I am wearing jeans but can u giv me a style and colour of top which would go nicely? Text back soon.

Example 2:
What did da mum biscuit say when da baby biscuit got hit by a car? Oh crumbs.

Example 3:
THANX 4 THE GR8 PARTY!XXX

Example 4:
FANX 4 BEIN A MAZIN MAG AN AVEIN COOL BANDS LIKE PAPA ROACH UR DA BEST.

Example 5:
Jus 2 tell my m8 congrats u no I like him really! PS: Watch out 4 da camel!

In a campaign for *Top of the Pops* magazine, a publication which has a similar (if slightly younger) target readership to *J17*, Aerodeon aimed to reproduce messages 'written in a style consistent with the text language of the target market, to reflect the familiar, hip tone of the medium'. This required analysis of the text language abbreviations in the text messages sent to the magazine by readers.

The following message was sent out during a Top of the Pops television broadcast featuring SClub7 and was clearly designed to appeal to the target market in terms of language and content:

TOTPMag2yrfone: Bradley S Club snogged 12 girls in 1 nite! Wait til UC wot other saucy secrets S Clubbers told us at TOTP this week. TOT PMag out Wed 7 June!

Another message in the campaign also illustrates the use of text shorthand:

TOTPMag2yrfone: Keepin U in touch with D l8est pop fun. Klik www.samanthamumba.com 4 cool Gotta Tell U ring! Her sngle out this wk – we rckn its wicked.

For Andrew Jones, the language used for text messaging by children and young adults is indicative of its tribal appeal. In an in-depth article for the *International Journal of Advertising and Marketing to Children* (January 2002) titled 'Wireless marketing: the linking value of text messaging', he outlined his views on how SMS relates to the 'neo-tribalism' of today's youth market:

We see common phrasing and abbreviations used by children who are in the same gang, follow the same pop group or read the same magazine. These secret codes that bind each community also protect them, just as table manners did for the Victorian upper classes. The codes are constructed in such a way that impostors are easily spotted. This can make it treacherous for brands, but for those that get it right there is respect. This is praise indeed for a youth brand.

The language young mobile users use when sending text messages is therefore not just a convenient way of shortening messages, although it is that as well; it is a means of establishing their place within the 'tribe'. However, while this tribal consciousness needs to be acknowledged by youth marketers, it does not apply – at least not to the same extent – for brands seeking to target a broader age range. But even so, text is a unique medium and the language used needs to be carefully considered. It is certainly no coincidence that the SMS campaigns that have achieved the best results have been aimed at carefully defined, niche audiences. After all, SMS is arguably the most intimate and personal communications medium. Adopting a unique, relevant language is the most obvious way to overcome the impersonality, which all too often is associated with new media marketing campaigns.

Case study: the *Guardian* SMS Poetry Competition

The *Guardian's* text message poetry competition was the first of its kind when it launched in March 2001, not only in the UK (where the paper is based) but also worldwide. As such it received widespread media articles, with feature articles on the competition appearing in *Time* magazine and *Wired.com* among many other publications.

Over a two-week period, *Guardian*-reading mobile phone users were invited to submit poems of under 160 characters (the maximum possible with a text message) by sending them to a special phone number. Over 7,500 poems were sent in, some using ordinary language, others interlaced with SMS shorthand. A prize of £1,000 was given for the best entry, with smaller cash prizes on offer for the runners-up. The competition was also noteworthy for its interactive element: the final shortlist of seven poems was texted to all entrants (one poem a day for seven days) so participants themselves were the ultimate judges.

In the introduction to the competition, participants were instructed that, 'This is a new literary form and it must be left to define its own parameters. In this competition the medium really is the message.' The contest also served as a way to introduce people to the relatively new medium. 'If you can't send a text message then now is the time to learn,' readers were told. 'It is probably the simplest of all the information age techniques to master.'

The winning entry, which came from Hetty Hughes, included various examples of SMS shorthand:

Txtin is messin/mi headn'me englis/try2rite essays/they all come out txtis/gran not plsed w/letters shes getn/swears I wrote better b4 comin 2 uni.& she's african.

'Text messages combine the pleasures of reading and writing with instantness and a handy little gadget,' said poet Andy Wilson, one of the competition judges. 'Most importantly, text messages let us think about our reply, choose our words carefully.' His belief that 'having rules and barriers to overcome is very liberating creatively,' certainly holds true for the mobile marketer. After all, being able to create a message which, in the space of 160 characters, is able to attract relevant interest in what you are promoting, is an art in itself.

Perhaps the key lesson marketers can take from the *Guardian* contest is the level of engagement it required. The role of the participants did not end when their poems were submitted. Towards the end of the competition all entrants were texted a message to remind them that, starting the next day, they would be sent one of the final seven poems every day for a week at around lunchtime for judging. In order for their vote to count, they were told to reply as soon as possible with a mark out of 10. Only those who responded to the first request were sent the remaining six entries.

Although the paper has not disclosed any readership increases from the telepoetry contest, the participation level was more than double the 3,000 entries the *Guardian* expected.

Mobile mentor: Anne de Kerckhove, Managing Director, 12Snap UK

Getting consumers hooked to mobile marketing

Texting is now a recognized cultural phenomenon, with its own spiky, vowel-free, onomatopoeic language. But as a marketing channel, the mobile is undeniably a medium in its infancy. And most brands and advertising agencies are still not using it to its full benefit. In order to gain consumer acceptance, mobile marketing campaigns must follow some key rules:

● *Permission*. Mobile communications are very personal exchanges, and, unlike e-mail, are largely disassociated from work. It is peer-to-peer communication in its purest form. Any unwelcome intrusion into this

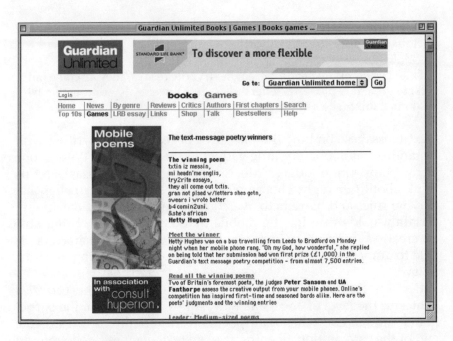

Figure 7.2 The *Guardian's* SMS Poetry Competition received widespread coverage

personal space runs a very strong risk of rejection. Thus, permission-based marketing is not only best-practice but rather the only effective strategy when using mobiles as marketing channels.

- *Targeting*. Campaigns must be targeted and tailored to the audience. The mobile phone is an extremely personal device and the make of phone, the fascia colour, its size, its ringtone are all extensions of an owners' personality. Therefore messages sent to consumers via the phone must be extremely relevant and targeted.

- *Value added*. The communication must be relevant and must add inherent value to the consumer. This can take the form of entertainment or exclusive access to goods and information.

- *Interactive*. Mobile marketing should engage consumers in a true two-way dialogue. 12Snap's research and practical experience have demonstrated that consumers love to talk back. The youth embrace brands in a new deeper way and are happy to display commercial logos on their phone as a sign of loyalty. But this new brand relationship implies the right to talk back to the brand.

Mobile marketing mechanics must be very simple. If the consumer does not get it the first time, he/she will never participate in the promotion again. Text messaging never came with a long list of instructions: it took off because it was intuitive and easy.

Running effective campaigns requires creativity and consumer focus, which often means adopting the spiky language of your target audience. Too many companies are relying on the novelty of the medium and generate very weak one-way-push campaigns with no creativity or interactivity. Instead we should be integrating IVR, voice and text based games, images and sounds to simple push campaigns!

There is no doubt that the mobile is a viable marketing channel for several target audiences. We believe we now have a responsibility to push the boundaries and live up to the full potential of the mobile, as long as we all keep communicating in the right language.

12Snap is Europe's leading provider of mobile marketing campaigns to big brands and media companies. 12Snap currently has 14 million aggregated permission-based opt-in users, making it the largest mobile marketing channel in Europe. Top global brands to have partnered with 12Snap include McDonald's, 20th Century Fox, Emap and Nestlé.

Last word

As advances in mobile technology gradually enable text messages to include audio, images and, eventually, streaming video, the need to fit everything into a 160 character message will evaporate. However, simple abbreviations and acronyms will persist as the habit of sending short messages back and forth is unlikely to disappear altogether. The fact that many people send abbreviation-filled messages which are way under the character limit also indicate that, luv it or h8 it, txtspk is here 2 stay.

eight

Integrating mobile campaigns

One of the reasons mobile marketing can prove to be so powerful is because, in an age when we are bombarded with marketing messages at every turn, a text message is still able to command our attention. Because it is interactive, and because it can reach us wherever we are, the mobile phone is the ultimate weapon available to the 21st century marketer. Of course, this weapon can blow up in your face, and frequently does, but when it is used with care and intelligence, it has the power to build mutually beneficial relations between a business and its customers.

So, if this is the case, why bother with more conventional forms of media at all? Well, tempting as it may be to concentrate on one medium at the expense of all others, this is not a practical solution. The fact is that even the most avid texters watch, read and listen to other media. To maximize your chances of reaching mobile users you must therefore adopt an integrated approach, in which each medium works off each other to create a stronger impact than any one could on its own.

Moreover, it is very difficult to conduct a responsible mobile marketing campaign without external media. After all, if you are only sending permission-based messages to opt-in subscribers, how are they going to hear about it in the first place? If you are to avoid sending spam, some form of cross-media activity surrounding a text message campaign is therefore inevitable. This chapter looks at some of the most common text message/traditional media alliances.

Text messaging and television

On the face of it, text messaging and television have little in common. As a medium, text is two-way, personal and – even with the addition of multimedia – visually limited in size and format. While a text message is usually aimed at an individual user, television broadcasts its messages to the widest audience possible.

Despite, or perhaps because of, this considerable difference, text messaging and television work very well together. As television tries to adapt itself to the interactive age, the humble text message has become a most useful tool. The current trend for reality television, where viewers can influence the course of the programme (a trend initiated by *Big Brother*) lends itself well to text messaging. Typically, viewers are asked to text their vote by dialling a premium rate number either during or immediately after a programme. Texting is also used to encourage interactivity on live television programmes, such as Saturday morning shows aimed at children. In 2001, many of these shows were receiving more text 'shout outs', than e-mails, letters and voice calls combined.

There are even entire shows devoted to text messaging. In the UK, the BBC ran a 'text night' and packed the schedule with shows devoted to mobile users. MTV's *Video Clash* has gone even further. The entire content of every show is dictated by the flood of messages it receives. Viewers are offered a choice of two artists – for instance, U2 and Missy Elliot – and vote for their video of choice. The results are then shown in real time, so when Missy fans see U2 is winning they are prompted to recast their vote. As MTV makes money on each message, they are not too worried about multiple voting. Indeed, rival fans are invited to participate in 'head to head' text bouts. If that wasn't enough to keep the viewers' thumbs busy, the *Video Clash* show also scrolls text dedications across the screen. Judging the show simply in terms of text message response, it is a phenomenal success. Each 45-minute show typically generates 25,000 messages.

The television broadcasters don't just rely on incoming traffic, either. Many choose to send schedule reminders to mobile users.

For instance, Channel 5 used an opt-in SMS campaign to generate interest in its 9pm blockbuster films. The carrot used to get subscribers was a competition for £20,000 based on a series of questions. The competition was promoted via television trailers, during which viewers were encouraged to sign up by sending a text message. Having opted in, viewers received a weekly reminder about a forthcoming movie. Then, having watched it, they were sent another text message with a competition question based on the movie. In other words, if viewers wanted to enter the competition they needed to watch Channel 5. And, according to the marketing firm that carried out the campaign (Flytxt), that is exactly what they did. An 80 per cent response rate for each question was reported, indicating just how powerful the text/television combination can be.

Case study: television takes a break for SMS link-up

Nestlé Rowntree, one of the world's largest packaged food manufacturers and 12Snap, the leading European mobile marketing company, capitalized on the power of the text/television combination when they worked together in the summer of 2001, linking an SMS text messaging competition to a Nestlé television commercial for KitKat. The SMS message announcing the transmission details was delivered to 12Snap's userbase, which stored the details of thousands of phone users, a day before the advertisement premiered.

The SMS drive continued 30 minutes prior to the premiere, when 12Snap's users were texted again with a question relating to the content of the advertisement. The first 50 correct entrants won a month's supply of KitKat and all were notified of the outcome via text. The response rate for the UK campaign, combined with similar success in Germany, 'far exceeded' all their expectations. It enabled them to recover interesting demographic data from their target market and convinced Nestlé of the importance of mobile marketing.

'This campaign demonstrates how a modern, direct media such as SMS can complement a traditional, passive media such as television,' said Marketing Manager Ros Horne, at the time of the campaign. 'Another of the great strengths of the SMS element of the campaign is that it enables us to reach the elusive 18–25-year-old market. Men and women receive a separate creative execution to enhance initial response. Analysis of the different response rates overall will enable us to build up a good picture of the impact of this type of advertising on the different sexes.'

Anne de Kerckhove, Managing Director of 12Snap agreed. 'In the last two years texting has touched everyone's life in the UK, particularly the youth audience. For a major brand like Nestlé to embrace the communications abilities of modern technology signifies a huge step forward in traditional marketing methods. 12Snap are at the very edge of these latest developments.'

Print media

Text numbers are often included in print advertisements to capture consumers' interest from the second they see a product or service that is relevant to them. This helps to activate a campaign and maximize the chances of brand recall.

Print media are particularly suited to SMS because they are able to give clear details of what mobile users should do, and the number they should contact. It is certainly no coincidence that some of the earliest companies to take mobile marketing seriously were magazine publishers such as Emap. Indeed, many magazines now offer some form of ongoing SMS campaign. Whereas initially it was only youth sector magazines (such as *Top of the Pops*, *Sugar*, *J17* and *Mizz*) that took an avid interest, now magazines targeting an older readership have also got in on the act.

For instance, *Men's Health* magazine, which targets men between the age of 25 and 44, runs a highly successful service called the 'Belly Off Club' in conjunction with Flytxt. Billed as 'the world's first weight-control text-messaging service', it offers daily calorie-conscious menus tailored to readers' specific tastes and local amenities. Such a degree of personalization, for obvious reasons, is not possible via the magazine itself, particularly considering its wide readership of 883,000.

Figure 8.1   *Men's Health* helps mobile users lose their belly

As the *Men's Health* service has already been recognized as one of the most successful SMS/print media partnerships in the UK, it is worth looking at exactly how it works. According to Flytxt director Pamir Gelenbe, 'this is ultimately a revenue-generating exercise for *Men's Health*'. But if it is, where is the revenue being generated from? Unlike other SMS services, *Men's Health* is not pushing its own products and no reverse billing system is in place (although Gelenbe says that future versions will include reverse billing payments). As *Men's Health* tells its readers, 'You do not pay for any of the text messages you receive'. However, they do point out that the service 'is subsidized by your initial call to your premium-rate phoneline'.

The premium rate phoneline charges users 75p per minute to complete an automated response questionnaire about their eating habits and access to local supermarkets. While such a high rate could act as a deterrent, *Men's Health* clearly states the length of the average call (2.5 minutes). Other possible deterrents are also combated within each month's issue, by providing answers to frequently asked questions. This is a good tactic for any mobile marketer to use, when trying to sway hesitant mobile users. Here are some examples of the *Men's Health* FAQ list, some of which relate to all SMS campaigns:

Is it easy to cancel my membership?
   Easy and quick. Just reply STOP to any of our messages and we'll cancel all future text messages to that mobile.

Will I get 'spammed' with an endless stream of marketing messages?
   You won't get a single one. Club rules don't allow your mobile number to be given or sold to any outside company. The only contact you'll ever receive is from *Men's Health*.

What if I don't like eating the choice you send me?
   We can't suggest anything you don't like because when you call to register, we'll ask – in detail – what foods you're happy to eat, and what you wouldn't touch with a barge-pole.

What if the shops have sold out of that day's suggestion?
   We've though of that. Every daily text menu carries a DIY option as well – a lunch that you can have made up at any independent sandwich shop.

I've been in a coma for two weeks – have I missed the start date?
   No. Our lunchtime menu system works on a loop, so it doesn't matter which day of the month you make your registration call, you'll still receive a month's supply of weekday lunch menu suggestions.

Of course, sending recipes via SMS causes inevitable problems. Not least among these is the fact that a single text message cannot exceed 160 characters – including spaces. *Men's Health* got around this problem by using shorthand where necessary, and then explaining the abbreviations to readers in the magazine (S/W for sandwich, CHSE for cheese, CHCKN for chicken, and so on). They also provide a full glossary of all the terms on their Web site.

To sum up, here are the key lessons to be learnt from this hugely successful SMS/print service which can be applied to other cross-media campaigns:

- *Personalization.* Personalization is one of the reasons behind the Belly Off Club's success. There are thousands of different options available, making it one of the most sophisticated text messaging campaigns to date. As Flytxt Carsten Boers commented, 'The personalized nature of the information that readers will be receiving makes the mobile the perfect device for this campaign'.

- *Consistency.* The messages are sent on a daily basis at exactly the same time.
- *Timing.* The messages deliver lunchtime menus at an appropriate time (10.30–11.30 am).
- *Ongoing revenues.* Once users have dialled the premium number to register, they then receive free messages for a month. When the month period is over they need to dial the number again. Having already got into using the service for the past 30 days, the incentive to rejoin is high.
- *Further potential.* Any cross-media SMS campaign should be able to evolve according to user demand. As Men's Health wanted to make the offer widely accessible in the first place, they decided not to include reverse-billing. However, if it continues into the long term, this could be incorporated. Furthermore, the aim is to sell the service to third parties in the future and as I write this, Flytxt and *Men's Health* are holding talks with supermarkets which might be interested in sponsoring the service.

Case study: *Top of the Pops* magazine text club

Although *Top of the Pops* (TOTP) magazine is the market leader for teenage pop news, it is not complacent about the fact. Indeed, during the period July–December 1999, *TOTP* saw its lead over *Smash Hits* (its main rival) reduced from 150,000 to 127,000. In addition, the most popular teen title, *Sugar* magazine, increased its lead over TOTP from 50,000 to 62,000.

1999 was also the year when tens of thousands of British teenage girls were adopting text messaging as a new, fun way to communicate. They started to take their phones everywhere with them and newspapers ran features about how schools had started insisting on phones being switched off during lessons. Aware of this trend, *TOTP* magazine – in conjunction with Aerodeon – launched the

UK's first text pop gossip service as a permission-based, relationship marketing tool in 2000. No database existed of mobile phone numbers, so a process needed to be designed for readers to submit their numbers. This needed to be easy and to allow sufficient demographics to be collected for subsequent profiling.

A text registration process was created whereby readers were invited to send a text message to a phone number printed in the magazine, and to include their date of birth, gender and postcode. This avoided the need for a second medium, such as coupons or the Web, and meant that the reader's phone number could be automatically captured, thereby eliminating user error. According to Aerodeon, it also provided an opportunity for readers to communicate with the magazine from their phones in their own text language. This was the first text registration service in the UK. Readers were invited to 'text register' and in exchange were promised the latest pop gossip delivered to their phone. The response to the half page offer was extremely high, with 10 per cent of readers with mobile phones registering within the first week.

The first text message was broadcast on 2 June during the *Top of the Pops* show in order to maximize the media impact. After the transmission, hundreds of readers sent spontaneous text messages of thanks into *TOTP*. The subsequent ABC audit data showed that *TOTP* magazine had extended its lead over *Smash Hits* and was closing the gap with *Sugar* magazine.

The text targeting incorporated not just the demographics, but also the timing of the broadcast. Messages often included information on bands featured on that evening's *Top of the Pops*. As with most successful campaigns there was a viral element, and the service was communicated via word of mouth. Multiple registrations have been received from the same phone being passed round the playground, and each time a message was broadcast there was a flurry of new registrations.

'Children are placing an increasing emphasis on the linking value of products and services,' says Aerodeon's Andrew Jones. 'This is a major reason why text messaging has been so readily adopted by children and provides key insight into how text can best be used by marketers. Linked communities, or tribes, share information in their own language, which if correctly treated can provide marketers with a credible basis for communications.'

Figure 8.2   The *Top of the Pops* Web site is used to collect further mobile user information

SMS, MMS and the Internet

Text messaging, whether via SMS or the multimedia MMS, is highly compatible with the Internet. Indeed, many of the leading Web portals have launched SMS services for instant messaging via gateways on their sites, along with downloadable ringtones. Internet banking sites offer updates and transactional notifications via SMS. In the corporate world, Intranet applications can leverage SMS for sales staff support, CRM, inventory updates, broadcasting services, e-mail gateways and product delivery enquiries.

For marketers, the synergy between the Internet and text messaging often proves irresistible. One of the most common ways SMS and the Web come together is when a text message directs recipients to a Web site for further information. Such a tactic not only has a practical purpose – it is often impossible and almost always unwise to express much information via text – but also significantly increases the chances of brand recall. Furthermore, for e-commerce sites it enables marketers to direct each recipient to a point of purchase.

With MMS this synergy becomes stronger still. Indeed, the vast store of multimedia content and streaming services on the Internet has been identified as one of the key catalysts for MMS success. For marketers, MMS makes it possible to push active content, such as that used on Web sites, via mobile devices.

Perhaps the most significant way text messaging and the Internet or desktop PC work together is in the actual implementation of a campaign. Indeed, there are a growing number of software products aimed at making life easier for businesses who use text messaging. For a selection, and some possible free downloads, visit the South African Cellular site (www.cellular.co.za/download_free_sms_software.htm).

One of the most popular services so far has been RedRock's TextNow, which enables users to send messages via a dial-up modem, a mobile phone, or an Internet connection using RedRock's server. At present this server connects to 240 mobile networks in over 90 countries. Most beneficial of all is the fact that it enables users to send one message to a list of numbers. In addition, TextNow provides an SMS character count and enables you to check on each message's program. However, if you decide to use RedRock's SMS server via the net, there is a charge per message, which varies according to the quantity you decide to send. For the latest information on pricing and a free trial download, visit Redrock's UK site (www.redrock.co.uk) or Redrock US (www.redrocktechnologies.com).

One example of a campaign that inventively used text messaging and Internet technology in unison was set up by mobile messaging company Upoc for Capitol Records and rock band Radiohead. The campaign – designed to keep Radiohead fans up to the minute on summer releases, concerts, Webcasts, and any other happenings of interest – sends fans voice messages and clips from tracks and was designed to integrate with an Internet strategy as well. For example, an Internet e-mail about an upcoming appearance could be reinforced on the day of the appearance with an SMS text message.

SMS and outdoor advertising

The following Irish examples illustrate the compatibility of SMS with outdoor media.

PosterTxt

PosterTxt is a permission-based direct response service set up by outdoor advertising giant JCDecaux which links clients' posters and Ireland's mobile phone users. According to Puca the result is 'an innovative marketing tool which is fun for consumers yet provides detailed statistics and a measure of campaign effectiveness to advertisers'. Its most dynamic use has been to encourage brand loyalty and access specific audiences, especially young audiences, by using their language and their means of communication.

The technique facilitates the use of outdoor advertising sites in interactive campaigns by way of integrated wireless marketing components. Consumers are encouraged to send text messages in response to poster communication and in the process will provide advertisers with valuable customer data. PosterTxt provides a range of tailor-made products including competitions, logo downloading, information dialogues, m-coupons and shopping coupons. Ultimately, it enables brands to plan street campaigns with integrated wireless marketing components: Bacardi was the first brand to use this service.

Txt 2 Win poster campaign

Irish marketing firms Viacom Outdoor and Rtn2Sndr came together in June 2001 for a 'Txt 2 Win' campaign. The aim was to judge the effectiveness of SMS as a means of direct response to traditional advertising. Six sheet posters were strategically placed at stations for commuters on the DART line in Dublin to see. They had the chance to win free cinema tickets by sending the answer to a question to Rtn2Sndr's SMS server. The question was 'By what name is James Bond better known?' Over 2,000 commuters responded correctly to the campaign over a two-week period. Winners were alerted by text message and replied with their name and address to be sent tickets (10 pairs of tickets were given away every day).

The campaign also generated press interest from the *Irish Marketing Journal* and the *Irish Times*. 'We were delighted with the effectiveness of the first Viacom Outdoor campaign. SMS is a superb means of direct response for advertising, especially for transport advertising where people are experiencing "dead-time"', said a spokesperson from Viacom Outdoor. 'We are excited at the possibilities that come from adding SMS interactivity to traditional advertising, and the SMS and fulfilment sides of the campaign were very efficiently managed.' As a result of the campaign Viacom Outdoor retained Rtn2Sndr to manage the SMS capability in the future.

The reason for text

There are a number of reasons why marketers incorporate a text message element into their media campaigns. Here are just some of them:

- *Instant feedback.* Because mobile users text as soon as they see an ad – whether it is on television, radio, the Web or in a magazine – companies can get instant feedback on a campaign's success.
- *Two-way marketing.* If you are promoting a product or service via traditional media, the consumer remains passive. By providing a strong call to action through SMS, marketers can transform a campaign into a two-way dialogue.
- *Localization.* Broadcast and print media often offer few opportunities to localize message content. This can change via SMS as a national campaign can be created with a local focus. Mobile users can send a text message containing details of where they live. The text reply can then be tailored to include local details, such as where their nearest outlet is.
- *Further information.* A text message may include further information or details of a special offer.
- *Revenue generation.* Of course, one of the most obvious reasons to use SMS is as a source of revenue generation. Although reverse billing is only advisable for certain activities, SMS can be used to promote other products. Premium rate phone numbers can also add a useful revenue stream.

SMS and radio

As the following UK case studies testify, radio broadcasters are starting to embrace SMS.

Galaxy Radio's Text Maniac's Club

Chrysalis Radio's first interactive text message campaign, developed by Flytxt on local dance music radio station Galaxy 105 (based in Yorkshire), aimed to build a relationship with Galaxy's listeners, who were offered the chance to win a free annual cinema pass if they joined the 'Text Maniacs' club. Galaxy also wanted to build a database of listeners for future communication and feedback. Trailers ran on Galaxy throughout June 2001 inviting listeners to join the club by sending an SMS with their postcode. Potential subscribers were also tempted with a range of special offers from Galaxy's approved partners. The total database size from the first phase of the campaign was 15,000. As Galaxy has an average of 80,000 listeners, this was 20 per cent of its average listener database. Furthermore, the Galaxy campaign illustrates just how fast mobile users respond to broadcast media. Ninety-five per cent of the responses came immediately after trailers, while the other 5 per cent were attributed to viral marketing.

Txt2Air

Quartez, the mobile messaging provider, has created 'Txt2Air', an SMS service which allows broadcasters to interact with their audiences. National radio station talkSPORT was the first to sign-up to the service, using SMS to canvas opinion on topics discussed on the radio station. As the station's frequency is 1089 am and 1053 am, listeners would simply text the number 8 1089, which ties in with the company's brand to provide opinion. The texts received are converted to e-mail and seamlessly integrated with the talkSPORT Web site (www.talksport.net) and the monitoring system in the studio.

'The 'Txt2Air' service can be set up very quickly for any broadcaster, giving radio and television stations another medium with which to create more interaction with their audience to provide opinion and polls,' explains Gary Andersen-Jones, managing director of Quartez. 'More than 950 million text messages are sent each month, which is an indication of the nation's obsession with text messaging, and the newest service aimed at broadcasters is a continuation of our roadmap for media companies to extend and market their brands via SMS.' According to Bill Ridley, project executive at talkSPORT Radio, talkSPORT wanted to have more interaction with their audience using a method that was simple and easy to use for their listeners. 'Our listeners are now able to interact with the programme via phone, e-mail and text.'

Classic FM

Classic FM, the country's largest commercial radio station, launched the first ever online catalogue of classical mobile ringtones with a range of especially composed tunes ranging from Handel's *Queen of Sheba* to *Prokofiev's Dance of the Knights*. Around 3.4 million of Classic FM's listener base already own a mobile phone, which equates to roughly 29 per cent of all mobile phone owners in the UK. Classic FM Web master, Rob Weinberg, said, 'We pride ourselves on demystifying classical music, and bringing it to a much wider audience. Mobile ringtones are a perfect example of bringing classical music into people's everyday lives. I think ringtones are going to be very popular for Classic FM, and a great way to pilot other mobile services like SMS alerts.'

The Classic FM ringtones were available from September 2001 at a cost of £3 each. Tunes available included the Classic FM Hall of Fame favourites selection, famous movie sound tracks, plus five special edition Classic FM jingles. Classic FM expects to expand the selection of ringtones available.

SMS: the perfect back channel

'It's probably no coincidence that most successful operators of mobile traffic are those that use the mobile as the back channel,' says Ray Anderson, CEO of Bango.net (a company which helps businesses promote and get paid for mobile content). Indeed, most of the really successful text message campaigns have not used the mobile as the starting point. 'Whether it is voting for pop charts, entering television competitions, joining clubs in the newspapers, or responding to chocolate bar promotions, the stimulus is usually offline,' says Anderson. The reason for this, aside from the obvious issue of spam, which is discussed elsewhere, is because the mobile device is the perfect response tool.

As with the Internet, SMS works best as a 'pull' medium. By integrating it with other media, this pull potential can be fully realized, enabling users to feel in total control over their mobile device, rather than being faced with an invasion of their personal space (and it is important to remember that this is how people see their mobile devices). After all, says Anderson, 'a mobile phone is a life support system, it is not a mind control device'.

Exploiting the full media potential

Another way in which offline and online media can be used in conjunction with text messaging is through PR. Text messaging is the PR person's dream, as news and feature editors can't seem to get enough of SMS stories.

Indeed, the publicity some campaigns have managed to generate has had a far more positive marketing effect than the campaigns themselves. Of course, there is a law of diminishing returns at work here: the more accustomed people become to the whole text messaging phenomenon, the less likely they are to guzzle up stories explaining it. But even so, technological advancements mean that new ways of text messaging will continue to occur way into the future. Furthermore, if the premise of your campaign is imaginative enough to win over potential customers who have never heard of you before (and if it isn't, why are you bothering?), it should also be imaginative enough to stand out in an inbox full of press releases.

Some of the PR-worthy SMS campaigns so far have included the New York Celebrity Sightings service, the *Guardian's* SMS Poetry Competition, Guinness's Interactive Treasure Hunt game and Pepsi's 'Text 2 the Max' campaign.

Product promotion

It is no coincidence that some of the largest responses for text message campaigns have occurred when SMS promotions have been placed on products. Indeed, many major brands have shown their confidence in mobile marketing by using their products as 'SMS prompts'.

Pepsi's 'Text 2 the Max' campaign involved placing details of the SMS-based promotion on 400,000 bottles of Pepsi Max across Ireland and Northern Ireland. Cadbury's, however, went even further when it decided to promote an SMS-based competition on 65 million of its chocolate bars.

Mobile mentor: Jeremy Wright, Co-Founder, Enpocket

Complementary media

Whatever other medium is used, wireless is a natural complement for the simple reason that mobile phones are an always held, always on personal communication device. Experience with SMS activity linked to television campaigns has shown that consumers readily respond by SMS to a television call-to-action, or react positively to SMS follow-up to television activity.

In this respect wireless has a way to go in developing as a sophisticated research and response mechanism for above-the-line campaigns. Just think how the relative merits of Web site reference and telephone questionnaires can combine with the smart use of WAP and SMS targeted to television campaign viewers.

And just consider how a really well targeted, personal offer delivered to a customer at the right time in the right place, say at the shopping mall on a Saturday morning, can tie with a major media launch campaign for a new high interest, high value product.

Jeremy Wright is Co-Founder of Enpocket, the first UK wireless media sales house.

Last word

Many of the lessons for mobile marketing can be taken from the Internet. For instance, when the Web was first embraced by marketers in the 1990s, it was seen as a completely unique medium. Many new firms were established online, with little thought for offline media and 'real world' sales channels. Many offline firms that set up Web sites did so with the words 'brand integration' far from their minds. Instead they created parallel businesses, often with entirely different domain names. The sites they built were designed for this miraculous new breed of consumer – the Internet shopper. No one knew exactly what this strange species looked like, because they remained mysteriously invisible, lost in the realms of cyberspace. The only thing that could be ascertained with any certainty was the fact that the principles of traditional, offline marketing no longer applied. All you needed was a fantastic name, a state-of-the-art multimedia Web site (who cares if no-one has the technology to access it?), and a 20-page registration form. Once this was all in place these new Internet shoppers would be spending their cybercash like there was no tomorrow. Why bother with traditional media when, by the year 2002, we would all be downloading our books and magazines from the Internet and watching television from our laptops?

Of course, it hasn't happened like that. By the time people fully realized that Internet consumers and those two-legged creatures you see walking down the high street were actually the same species, it was too late. Those that did survive the downturn did so by adopting an integrated 'clicks and mortar' approach, in which the Internet was recognized as a valid sales channel and form of marketing media, but not the only one.

For mobile marketers not to fall into the same trap, it is necessary to understand that mobile users do not exist in a vacuum. They are surrounded by marketing messages beaming at them from a variety of different media. Furthermore, marketers must be able to integrate SMS into a broader, cross-media campaign in order to create the level of awareness required for a mobile user to subscribe to a text message service.

nine

The global message

The uses and abuses of text messaging vary between cultures and continents. In some countries SMS has been around for years, while in others it is only just starting to take off. This chapter explores some of these differences by looking at some of the imaginative ways people are using SMS worldwide. Particular attention will be paid to the United States, a market which has shown strong SMS potential, but where barriers to mass adoption still remain. In his contribution to this chapter, Marco Argenti, one of Italy's leading wireless experts, explains why he feels 'the future of SMS is North America'.

Text messaging: a global phenomenon

In Britain text messaging has rapidly become the communications medium of choice for many adults and children. School kids text each other their exam results, shy students send flirty texts across crowded dancefloors and lovers send intimate 'sex texts' when they are away from each other. Text messaging has even managed to save lives. It's not just Britain either. Throughout the world, people are finding increasingly imaginative uses of text messaging. When a woman was stranded on the Indonesian coast, she sent her boyfriend an SMS SOS on her mobile. The boyfriend, who was quietly enjoying a drink in his local pub at the time, managed to alert the relevant coastguard station, which sent out a rescue vessel.

In 2001, police in Amsterdam started to clamp down on mobile phone theft by using SMS. When a phone theft was reported, the Dutch police would send the following text message every three to five minutes: 'Warning. This is a stolen telephone, using it is a criminal offence.'

In Ireland, female students under the age of 24 have so far proved to be the most committed texters. 'They love to gossip and text is a great way to do it,' says Bettina MacCarvill, a Senior Analyst at the Dublin-based consultancy firm Amarach Consulting. In Germany, the country which leads the European market, mobile users are sent instalments of the world's first SMS soap opera, albeit for a small fee. In the Philippines in 2000, opposing troops were sending each other abusive and demotivating text messages on their mobile phones while in battle. And in Singapore, text messaging has turned on the one population segment which made it popular in the first place – teenagers. One school there sends text message alerts to parents when their teenage children play truant.

Perhaps it is in New Zealand that the most imaginative use of SMS has so far occurred. Every Spring, frost alert messages are sent to grape growers, in order to help protect and preserve the quality of future New Zealand wines. The country's Meteorological Service launched the first frost alert service in 2001, delivering a short SMS message to grape growers twice a day to give the grower more information on which to base costly decisions.

One reason why text messaging has taken off in so many areas is because it is cheap. For instance, in Finland (the country which has the highest concentration of SMS users) sending an SMS message costs half the price of making a voice call. Cost also explains, at least partially, why text messaging has been slower to take off in the United States than elsewhere. Although most of the main US telcos have offered SMS since 2000, uptake was initially very slow. 'One reason for the slow US uptake is that people in the United States pay per minute charges for cell phone services, whether they make or receive a cell phone call or send or receive a text message,' explained Elisa Batista in a *Wired.com* article titled 'Mobile messaging: bot in the USA'.

Another reason why Europe and Asia have soared ahead of the United States in the SMS stakes has to do with the technical standards that enable message transmissions. Whereas these standards are relatively uniform elsewhere, in the United States things are different. The dominant standard to send data via a wireless

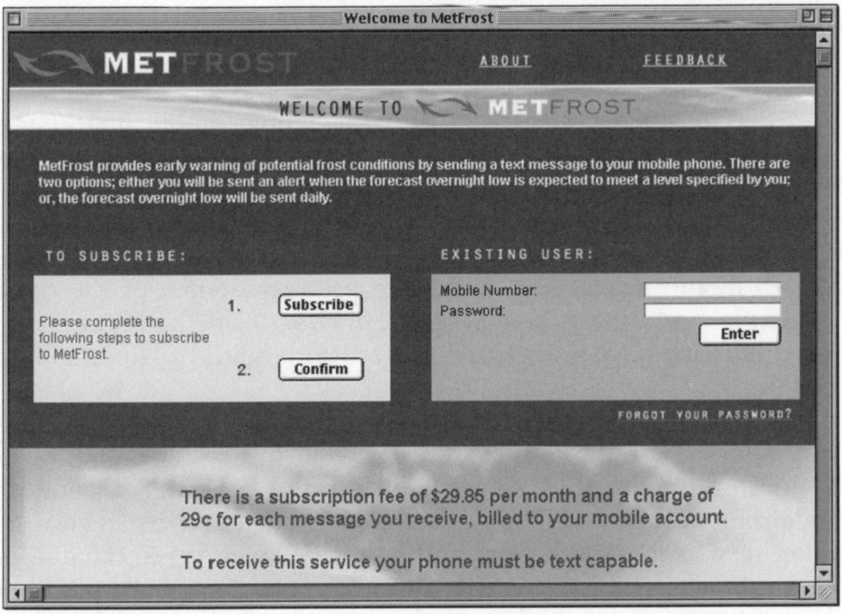

Figure 9.1   Winegrowers beat the frost thanks to this metero-logical service

network is referred to as the Global System for Mobile Communications (GSM). As GSM is not the dominant standard in the United States, the 'global' bit is rather misleading. Operators in the United States, unlike their European counterparts, have been working with a variety of conflicting wireless systems. In other words, US users have been more tied to their operator than they have been in other parts of the globe.

Developments by companies such as Ericsson, Alcatel, Motorola, Siemens and Infospace are making the future look brighter for text messaging in the United States. The work towards an improved SMS standard which enables people to send text messages with attachments is particularly encouraging. Indeed, as DADA's Marco Argenti argues in his contribution to this chapter, other barriers facing SMS in the United States, are starting to be dismantled. How soon text messaging based on SMS services is able to replicate its success in Europe and Asia in the United States remains to be seen, however.

The operator's perspective

In order to get a better picture of the whole mobile marketing landscape, it is important to understand where exactly the operators fit in, and how they benefit. Firstly, it is worth noting that the situation varies considerably from continent to continent. In Asia, operators such as NTT DoCoMo have so far played the most active role in mobile marketing, and have produced some of the most profitable models (for them at least). In Hong Kong and Singapore, the operators have even used advertising funds to finance free airtime.

In Europe, operators are also starting to take mobile marketing very seriously. Indeed, they have been using text messaging to communicate with their customers since the 1990s. UK Operators Vodafone, Orange and BT Cellnet also play an active role in encouraging responsible marketing, and have all signed up to the guidelines established by the MMA, although none have yet forbidden the sending of unsolicited, mass messages via their networks. They do, however, adhere to these guidelines in their own marketing practice. Financially, they have benefited considerably from gathering in the revenues from the SMS bulk broadcast rates they charge marketers and SMS providers. In the United States, operators tend to have a less active role as they gain nothing from text-message broadcasts. Instead, as we shall discuss, they charge mobile users to receive these messages.

In a 2001 report from Probe Research, entitled 'Wireless advertising: start-up profiles and projections', author Ann Lynch expressed her belief that many operators are likely to miss out. As she states in the report, 'Carriers have much to gain – in terms of revenue sharing, service fees charged to advertisers, royalty fees, commissions on transactions with a successful sale – but will surely miss the boat if they don't get involved!'

Mobile mentor: Robert Jesty, Arc Group

A brief guide to global market trends: a prediction

Mobile marketing is still at the early stages of its growth, but over the next few years it has the potential to play a leading role in the development of the mobile Internet. A number of major advantages are working in the favour of the mobile medium:

- The mobile device is highly personal and portable, and if the message is appropriately targeted, an advertiser can gain the user's undivided attention.
- Since the user is on the move, a message can de delivered closer in time to the point of action than by most other communication channels.
- The point of delivery can also be physically close to the action, for example in a shopping centre or at an airport. This has clear benefits for all kinds of sales promotion, and it is also invaluable for giving directions to a store or service outlet. Location technology will be an invaluable enabler for a whole new range of mobile marketing activities.
- Business models can be based on a personalized charging structure for each user, so that new services can be highly relevant and therefore valuable.

From the global viewpoint, Japan has taken an early lead in mobile marketing – not only because of the i-mode technology and infrastructure adopted by leading network operator NTT DoCoMo, but also because of innovative joint ventures between network operators and advertising agencies. ARC Group believes that the click to Web/click to e-mail/click to voice response model which is now in use at i-mode will in time be widely accepted in other regions around the world.

Mobile advertising and marketing has initially been targeted towards niche markets and the youth market, but will move into the mainstream over the next few years. After this take-off point, ARC Group forecasts that it will grow dramatically – reaching a figure of $12 billion globally by 2006.

Robert Jesty is Head of Projects at communications research company, Arc Group (www.arcgroup.com).

The view from Europe

There can be no denying that, when it comes to mobile technology and marketing, the European outlook is bright. A single mobile standard (GSM), a rapidly evolving infrastructure and more than a fair share of companies willing to push forward new technologies have certainly helped matters. Scandinavia, Italy and Germany have all witnessed a remarkable growth in mobile users (over 50 per

Mobile Marketing: World Revenues 2001–2006 ($ billion)

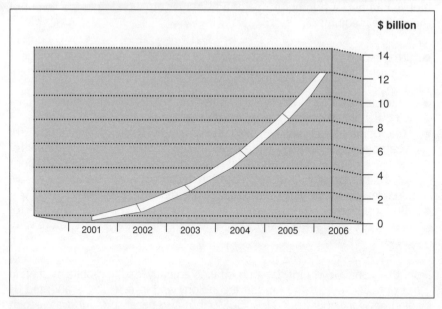

Figure 9.2 Mobile marketing: world revenues 2001–2006 ($ billion)

(Source: Arc Group)

cent of their populations own handsets). The UK, France and Spain are not far behind.

The investment in third generation (3G) technology, although costly for European operators in the short term, will ultimately pave the way for a user-friendly mobile Internet and possibly an end to the so-called digital divide. In a comprehensive report on 3G published by *eMarketer*, it was stated that '3G wireless technology will lead to a substantial increase in the number of Web access devices, even in countries where PC penetration remains low'. By 2005, 33 per cent of global m-commerce revenue is expected to come from Western Europe.

Case study: E-Taxi, Irish innovation

Some of the most imaginative uses of SMS text messaging are to be found in Ireland, the country which boasts one of the most text-active populations on the planet. City Cabs' E-Taxi service is a case in point. Instead of standing in the middle of the street flapping their arms in the rain, Dubliners can now send texts to an E-Taxi number. As this is a location-based service, the SMS message is automatically routed to the taxi which is closest to the pick-up point. The driver who takes the fare then calls the customer to confirm the booking.

The system uses 'triangulation' to find the nearest City Cabs taxi (which are all Mercedes-Benz, by the way), by locating the mobile phone mast a phone is getting its connection signal from. This mobile user can normally be pinpointed with up to 10 metres' accuracy. The innovation doesn't stop there, however. In the back of each taxi there is also a wireless modem swipe-card terminal which enables customers to pay electronically by credit card. At the time of writing, E-Taxi is also putting together an integrated SMS and Web portal to link customers to online and offline events.

Texting the United States

Although it is fair to say that the United States remains a PC culture, wireless penetration is continuing to rise. Furthermore, text messaging has also gained considerable appeal according to a study published by AT Kearney and Cambridge University. It found that, by the close of 2001, 12 per cent of those who owned Internet-enabled mobile phones were sending text messages – this was double the number of users just 12 months before. The study also discovered that 14 per cent of the United States' 120 million mobile users had an Internet enabled phone.

However, text messaging trends in the United States are still significantly different from those in Europe and Asia. For instance, the strongest interest in texting so far has been found in adults between 35 and 54 years of age. Furthermore, the AT Kearney/

Cambridge University study found that teenage usage was in decline, slipping 11 per cent in the space of a year.

While the overall figures are generally positive, US mobile users still have a few unavoidable deterrents. Some phones, for example, are not capable of both sending and receiving text messages. The main problem, though, is the lack of interoperability between the various standards in use throughout the country. As Marco Argenti explains in more technical detail below, measures are being made by the main carriers (who are adding more SMS-enabled products to their range), and the necessary technological advances are starting to get underway. It will be a while, however, before every obstacle is removed and text messaging can replicate its European and Asian success.

Mobile mentor: Marco Argenti, Managing Director of DADA's wireless sector

The future of SMS is North America

Is SMS ever going to take off in North America? That's the billion dollar question. It definitely hasn't yet: the phenomenon of text messaging is of abysmal proportions if compared to what it is in other parts of the globe such as Europe and Asia. Here are some of the most frequent explanations I hear:

● It's a 'cultural' thing.
● It's only popular where PC/Internet penetration is low as a substitute to e-mail.
● Americans don't like to triple-tap.
● Americans have alphanumeric pagers.

Yes, there may be some truth to some of those reasons. However, there are much more basic barriers to the adoption of SMS in North America, and the good news is they are bound to go away.

Reason number one is of a technological nature: it's a well known fact that Europe and most of Asia have standardized one of two mobile communications standards: GSM and CDMA. By contrast, there are at least five different, incompatible standards in North America: AMPS (the old analog standard, still very popular), TDMA, CDMA, iDEN and GSM. To make things worse, most carriers do not allow message roaming to and from other carriers, or even MO (mobile originated) text messages from their subscribers. Most phones do not even have a built-in text editor to compose messages with, and those that do lack basic usability aids. This alone would have been any potential killer application's killer. Imagine having e-mail, but only being able to communicate with users dialling up to the same ISP. Or being able only to receive, but not send messages.

Reason number two is related to the way carriers bill their subscribers in North America. Usually, the receiver is charged for the so-called 'airtime' that applies even if both callers are in the same location. Also, as Matt Haig has explained, receiving a text message costs money. In Europe, receivers never pay for incoming calls. In fact, some carriers apply a kickback, or 'recharge', for received calls, depending on their duration. The same applies to SMS. The closest analogy in the Internet world would be being charged extra for every e-mail being received, or better, for each Instant Messaging message received. The consequence would be that users only log on when strictly necessary (ie to send messages). This is exactly what many Americans do: turn their phone on only to make calls.

Fortunately, those barriers are falling. Judging from recent announcements and actual deployments, soon there will be two dominant standards across US carriers: CDMA 1x and GSM/GPRS. Both are intermediate steps to third generation technology, which will also see two standards being adopted, namely CDMA 2000 from Qualcomm and UMTS/WCDMA. The good news is that, by design, all carriers adopting one of the two standards will be interoperable both from a voice and a messaging standpoint. Even better, GPRS and CDMA 1x handsets are loaded with SMS-related features. The second barrier, the way carriers bill for a service, is a tougher one. But my prediction is that it's going to fall as well, driven by the necessity felt by the carriers to develop and promote value-add mobile data services in order to offset the investment made in upgrading their networks. The fact that text messaging could run on an IP-based bearer such as GPRS, making the receiver–caller distinction obsolete, is also a healthy sign for the future.

Just before Christmas 2001, I was driving on some American highway and noticed a billboard with Santa Claus showing a mobile phone. The phone's display read: 'MRRY XMAS'. The copy said 'Two Way Text Messaging, now available from …'. That reminded me of some ads I used to see in Europe a few years ago. I am not sure how many people actually exchanged greetings through SMS in America in 2001. In Italy alone, a country with a population of 60 million people, 270 million messages were sent on Christmas Day. At an average of 10 cents per message, that's a very merry Christmas for carriers throughout Europe. Can their American counterparts afford to miss out on such an opportunity?

At present Mario Argenti is one of the 50 members of the Commerce Partner Advisory Board of Microsoft. Managing Director of Wireless Solutions (a company controlled by DADA), Argenti, as a Managing Director, is responsible for DADA's wireless activities.

DADA is an independent Internet company quoted on the Italian Stock Exchange which supplies high-value-added network services and solutions both for business clients and consumer users. With a portfolio of more than

30,000 company clients, DADA operates through its four separate Business Units including Argenti's Wireless Services.

Established in Bologna in March 2000, Wireless Solutions SpA is one of the leading WASPs (wireless application service providers) in Europe and is the point of reference in the Italian market for the development and supply of Internet services integrated with mobile phone technology such as WAP, SMS, GPRS and UMTS. Independent Internet Company DADA, listed on the New Market, achieved control of Wireless Solutions on February 2001.

Last word

If marketers are targeting international markets, they need to understand the differences in how SMS is used. No two countries, even within Europe, follow exactly the same pattern. For instance, in some it is primarily a youth-based phenomenon; in others it is not. However, for all this global diversity, the principles of mobile marketing remain fundamentally the same. After all, unsolicited messages receive the same frown whether they are sent to New York or Kuala Lumpur.

ten

Implementing a campaign

While most of this book explores the mobile phenomenon and the principles marketers should adhere to in order to capitalize on it, this chapter addresses the practical issue of how to go about implementing a campaign. Software solutions will be looked at for those who want full creative control over a campaign, and the outsourcing option will also be covered. Two controversial, but extremely insightful, opinion pieces (from mBlox's Andrew Bud and XT Marketing's Richard England) are incorporated within the chapter, taking different views on the inhouse/outhouse debate.

The technological requirements

Although text messaging, particularly SMS, is a relatively simple technology for individuals to use, coordinating a text message marketing campaign to thousands of mobile users requires more sophisticated resources. Andrew Bud points out, 'Most mobile marketers have learned that do-it-yourself SMS delivery is a recipe for expensive disaster'. That does not mean, however, that you should hand everything over to a third party and forget about it. The best approach is to do what you can in house, and then outsource for those areas where you need assistance.

So what does a mobile marketing campaign involve? For most marketers, the easiest way to implement a campaign is to use software which enables messages to be composed on a computer or via a Web service and sent to various mobile users simultaneously. However, it is also important to realize that, owing to the two-way nature of text message campaigns, receiving and monitoring messages is as important as (if not more important than) sending them out. As well as a sophisticated back-end infrastructure, texting also requires adaptable front-end technology which understands how to interpret messages. After all, not every mobile user will respond to a campaign in the same way, even if he or she is told exactly what to do. For example, says Flytxt's chief executive Lars Becker, 'People will slightly misspell the codeword and not follow the instructions properly. You need to be flexible enough to cope with this.'

Mobile mentor: Richard England, Commercial Director, XT Marketing

Mobile marketing is in the house

As things currently stand, brand owners and their marketing agencies are outsourcing their mobile marketing campaigns for lack of internal expertise and capability. Initially specialist agencies such as ours were given almost total responsibility for the design, execution and live management of client campaigns. But as we look ahead, we are likely to see a major shift of control back towards brand owners and their agencies, as they take more interest in this new medium.

We will see many more milestone terrestrial television shows with mobile interactivity such as *Big Brother*, which continues to be sponsored by BT Cellnet. Led by powerful groups like Capital Radio and Chrysalis, the radio industry will also be making increasing use of mobile. In fact, it is hard to imagine a more powerful endorsement of a new medium than to witness the established media not only making space for it, but avidly adopting it as well.

If mobile marketing has become so popular with media owners, then it is bound to become increasingly popular with brand owners and their agencies. As we know from past experience, innovations that work for television audiences also work for advertisers. In this respect BT's sponsorship of *Big Brother* is a good case study. It was particularly apt as the campaign offered the company the dual benefits of promoting both its brand and a core service on offer.

As mobile marketing comes of age, marketing professionals will begin to take a much more hands-on role in the live management of mobile campaigns, especially as those campaigns are likely to be ever more closely associated with their other media activities in order to fully exploit the power of mobile interactivity. With the right mobile marketing tools, the UK's marketing agencies will at last be able to do what they do best: be creative.

XT Marketing is a mobile marketing solutions company offering services to marketers, agencies and network operators.

Software solutions

There are a variety of Web-based services which enable you to compose text messages from a desktop PC, such as those provided by Lycos and Orange Internet. However, if you are going for an in-house solution, it is preferable to install your own software, as Web services offer a limited range of support. There are a number of Windows-compatible software solutions aimed at making life easier for individuals and businesses with databases of mobile users. As well as helping you with mobile marketing to customers, these also enable you to keep in touch with other contacts, such as suppliers or employees.

A typical pay-for solution will normally include at least most of the following features:

- *Text messaging server.* A text messaging server enables you to manage any number of text messages to single or various destinations simultaneously.
- *Multiple messaging support.* If, as with the case of TextNow (see below), the software product supports the delivery of text messages via your Internet connection, via a connected GSM modem or via standard Windows dial-up modems, there is no need to purchase and install a separate digital modem.
- *Web management.* Support via a Web client allows any user with a Web browser to create, send and manage a message.
- *Application integration.* If the product is designed to be integrated with e-mail, CRM or contact management software then it is infinitely easier to manage a campaign.
- *Message monitoring.* The ability to check on each message's progress is essential if a campaign is to be monitored successfully.
- *Character count.* As text messages have character limitations,

character counts let you know when you have exceeded the limit.

● *Simultaneous delivery.* Some services enable you to submit messages to multiple recipients within a single dialled connection. This means that whatever type of access you have, message delivery can be almost simultaneous.

● *Phonebooks.* A phonebook facility enables you to store numbers, and some enable you to transfer data stored in other databases.

Among the most respected programs are Desoft's SMS Centre and SMS E-mail, and RedRock's TextNow. Although Desoft's software tends to be cheaper, and is perfectly suited to small lists, TextNow is aimed at a move corporate market. As such, it warrants specific attention.

TextNow

Billed as 'the wireless messaging solution for your business', it is important to realize that TextNow is not a standard marketing product as such but rather a multi-purpose business 'solution'. In other words, its general aim is to improve business functionality across the board, not just to help you with your marketing messages.

That said, TextNow's stated ability to 'reach customers instantly and accurately' as well as to 'generate immediate response' is highly attractive to any mobile marketer. Other features which can help the smooth flow of a mobile marketing campaign include the option of sending to one or thousands of recipients, and the ability to schedule the transmission time of messages. If that wasn't enough, TextNow also enables marketers to:

● include a personalized suffix with each message;
● use a friendly 'Reply to' option for message responses;
● integrate the product with e-mail and CRM applications;
● manage queued messages;
● secure user access;
● route, respond and react to incoming messages;
● store numbers in 'Private' and 'Global' phonebooks.

TextNow also deserves a brownie point not only for being Windows-compatible, but also for providing a user-friendly

Windows System tray which makes the TextNow Windows client immediately available.

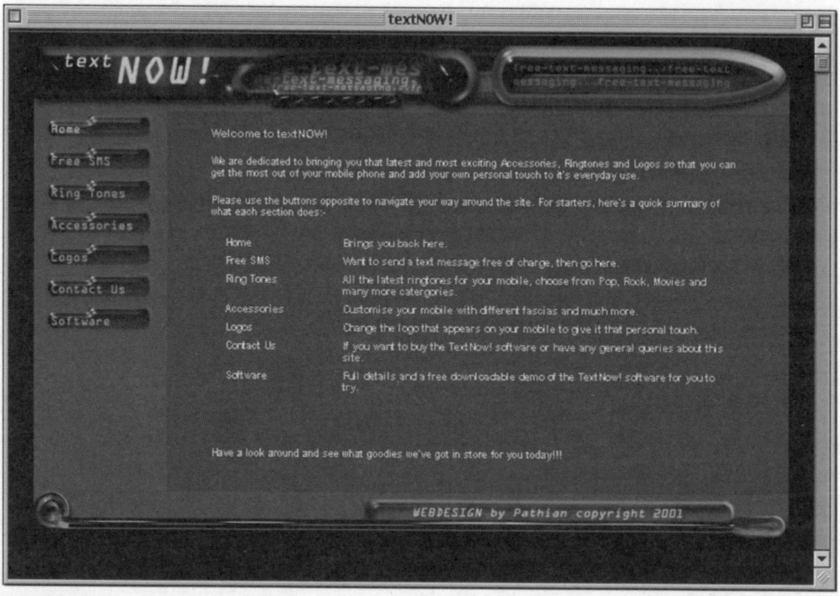

Figure 10.1   TextNow helps companies 'reach customers instantly and accurately'

TextNow enables every computer user on a local or wide area network to create and send text messages to any number of mobile phones or SMS-enabled devices. The message is delivered directly onto the customer's phone. Then, with Desoft's products, all customers need to do to respond is to return a message via their mobile phone.

Some TextNow versions also include a two-way text messaging option, which enables marketers to respond automatically to customer requests. 'For example, messages received containing the word 'MAP' could automatically respond to the sender's mobile phone with directions to your office,' says a RedRock spokesperson. 'A message containing a flight number could respond with details of delays or estimated time of arrival.'

RedRock has also identified the specific marketing benefits of its product in the TextNow brochure. 'If marketing is all about making it easy for your customer to respond, TextNow is your essential tool,' spouts the blurb. Although this, as with most hyperbolic sales material, needs to be read with a cautious eye, the fact that many UK marketers swear by this product should not be overlooked. Indeed, that it can help you to deliver an offer or promotion onto your customers' mobile phones and they can respond to you directly by pressing one button is itself a triumph.

So what's the downside? One small snag is that, at the time of writing, TextNow does not work with Microsoft Outlook. However, while this is a problem for businesses trying to streamline their overall communications, it should not affect the implementation of straightforward SMS campaigns. Anyway, RedRock does claim that it will soon support Microsoft Outlook. Of course, cost is another factor. Prices vary according to sophistication, and in the UK (where RedRock is headquartered) currently start at around £400. A 24-day trial version can be downloaded from the RedRock UK site (www.redrock.co.uk),

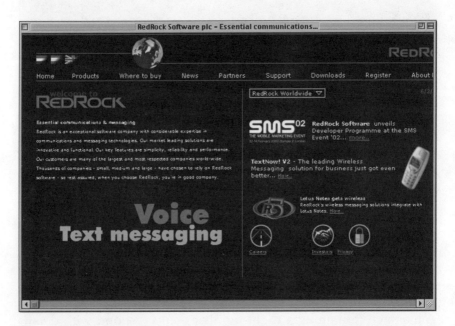

Figure 10.2 RedRock enables users to download a trial version of TextNow.co.uk

Other solutions

WebSMS (www.Websms.com)

Another popular product with big name mobile marketers is WebSMS, produced by UCP (Universal Communication Platform). Put simply, WebSMS is a bulk SMS sending application for companies and individuals. It enables subscribers to send text messages out to closed user groups direct from the Internet and has the ability to integrate two-way messaging and customer interactivity. WebSMS provides text messaging via the Internet and SMTP (e-mail to SMS) connections. It offers contact management and personalization of each message sent in a bulk mailing.

According to Christian Lutz, founder and chairman of UCP, 'WebSMS can be customized to provide interactive communication solutions, entertainment services like SMS games, high performance voting applications and messaging services'. Adidas is one of the high-profile companies to have already used WebSMS in a targeted mobile marketing campaign. (It used WebSMS for a targeted mobile marketing campaign coinciding with the Brit Awards.)

For more information visit the WebSMS Web site at www. websms.com.

Clickatell (www.clickatell.com)

South Africa-based Clickatell delivers bulk and individual SMS messaging services to more than 360 mobile phone networks worldwide and is one of few providers with direct access to the operators' relay centres. 'This gives us an advantage in sending bulk messages globally,' says the company's sales and marketing manager Bruce Watermeyer. What makes Clickatell different is its application programming interface, or API. 'This allows commercial clients to manage their messaging with constant support from the vendor, which is generally necessary for clients without their own technical support,' says Hainebach.

Clickatell's revenue comes mainly from the international market, and its customers use bulk SMS services as a cheap way of reminding customers of events and promotions. Watermeyer claims that Clickatell is the only company that can set up the messages so that they come from a named source, not a number. He also reports more than 105,000 international client registrations from close on 200 countries.

A user-friendly interface means the Clickatell Communicator service is one of the easiest to use and that any permission-based message can be sent to any mobile or fixed device at any time. Furthermore, Clickatell Communicator has a powerful 'mail-merge' facility. This allows the sender to broadcast bulk messages, while at the same time setting it up so that each message contains information relevant to specific recipients, such as their name or any other specified field. Uploading a group of recipients is also quite straightforward, making group messaging an easy task.

Once this has been done, all you need to do (in theory at least) is type the message and click 'send'. The bulk SMS tool is available for testing at www.clickatell.com/central/campaigns. Clickatell's range of user-friendly services has made them one of the leading players in the market; however, they stopped offering Web SMS services for free in March 2001.

iTouch (www.itouch.com)

iTouch offers a wide range of corporate SMS solutions, which enables marketers to add their own 'look and feel' to messages. These services include smart messaging (often used by media companies to build self-sustaining promotional tie-ins and generate income through revenue sharing with the telecom operator) and SMS alerts (letting you deliver a choice of content to your customers). WAP services are also available. iTouch's services provide organizations with an efficient, easy to use and cost-effective marketing tool for collecting competition responses and opinions, providing results, and setting up polls. On behalf of clients, iTouch can set up and run competition and vote lines, using a 'white-labelling' service.

NovelSoft (www.novelsoft.ch / www.sms-wap.com)

NovelSoft was the first company to provide network-independent global wireless messaging to mobile devices worldwide. Already covering more than 80 countries in Europe, Africa, the Middle East, and Asia/Pacific, NovelSoft's unique Internet-based messaging platform at www.sms-wap.com allows content providers, ASPs, and corporate accounts to distribute time-critical news like stock quotes.

ActivateXT

To meet the trend away from outsourcing and towards greater in-house control, XT Marketing has developed activateXT, a unique tool for marketers to manage every aspect of a campaign from design and testing to execution. ActivateXT's Web-based monitoring and reporting capabilities mean that campaigns can be rapidly modified when they are actually running. Once they have finished, marketing professionals are provided with post-campaign analytical feedback which enables them to effectively evaluate each of their activities.

Brand2Hand (www.brand2hand.com)

Brand2Hand is the managed mobile marketing service provided by London-based Luno Networks. Brand2Hand can provide Web registration and logo downloads from your Web site, customer database maintenance, text broadcast facilities and advanced campaign management functions. The Brand2Hand site enables you to trial the service for yourself. (You can download graphics and ringtones to your phone, trial the powerful automated campaign manager functions and learn more about the filtered broadcast services.)

Case study: the Cellar Society use Brand2Hand

The Cellar Society organize food and wine entertainment events, including the Grape Game Show, a wine tasting dinner and competition event, and Gastronomica, the unique food and wine game. Running these events involves a small army of staff to provide set-up, catering, serving and game hosting. The Cellar Society use Brand2Hand to communicate with their staff while they are organizing an event. The typical sequence of events starts with the Cellar Society selecting a list of potential staff for an upcoming event and sending them a short message asking them if they can work on a given date. From the positive responses that they get back, the Cellar Society then draw up a firm list of the staff for the event, and confirm the booking with them. Nearer to the date the Cellar Society then send out detailed instructions, explaining where the venue is, what time to get there, what to wear and any other special instructions. On the day they sometimes send another quick reminder. After the event the Cellar Society send a thank you message to the people who worked on the job.

'We often have several events to organize in parallel,' says Bertie de Rougement, Managing Director. 'Having such a convenient way to communicate with our people really helps us when the heat is on. Giving them clear, accurate and instant information about the events makes a great difference. We are also planning to use them for an RSVP service for invitations. We could use the full set of event management functions to handle invitations, response, tickets and reminders.'

Figure 10.3 Cellar Society uses Brand2Hand to help run successful events

Marketing agencies

Marketing and advertising agencies, particularly in Europe, have occasionally been criticized for their hesitant response towards text messaging. Although research findings have gone a long way in proving the effectiveness of mobile marketing campaigns –

response rates average at around 8 per cent according to Steve Wunker (anecdotal evidence suggests they can be sometimes as high as 40 per cent) – the larger advertising firms have so far been reluctant to jump on board.

In the UK during 2001 advertising firms came under particularly heavy fire for ignoring the rapid rise in text messaging experienced that year. However, the stand-offish attitude of long-established advertising firms was to a certain degree understandable. After many had rushed in to the Internet marketing space only to come away disillusioned, they were more likely to think twice before embracing another hyped new media phenomenon.

The fact that this risk factor was often gauged by junior members of staff made the move towards mobile marketing even more unlikely. However, the undeniable success of major SMS campaigns for global brands such as Pepsi and Harry Potter has now given many advertising firms a more positive view of mobile marketing. The other reason the giant agencies are having to take a closer look at text messaging is because of the growing rise of mobile marketing agencies.

Case study: Flytxt

Flytxt, the leading wireless marketing expert, was set up at the beginning of 2000 and has since built up an unrivalled list of blue chip clients and an extensive range of wireless marketing applications. Flytxt's technology platform and creative skills have been used to great effect in a number of wireless marketing campaigns, including a cutting-edge and award winning CRM campaign for *Smash Hits*, the biggest-ever SMS sales promotion campaign to date on behalf of Cadbury's and an innovative viral marketing campaign to create a pre-launch buzz around the release of Momentum Pictures' film *Get Over It*. Other clients who have benefited from Flytxt's services include Channel 5, Deutsche Bank and Carlsberg. Headquartered in the UK, Flytxt also has a presence in Germany. Flytxt has also built up key partnerships with respected media and advertising agencies and is a member of the MMA.

'From an advertiser's point of view, it's already a pretty complex world out there as far as marketing messages go,' says Anne de Kerckhove of mobile marketing firm 12Snap. 'Direct mail, print, television, radio are saturated. A lot of large corporates and, perhaps more importantly, their advertising agencies, don't know about the potential of mobile marketing yet.'

Others, such as Flytxt's head of client services Carsten Boers, believe that SMS is not 'sexy' or 'colourful' enough for many advertising firms to get excited about it. However, the arrival of multimedia text messaging (MMS) looks set to change this view.

Case study: 12Snap

'Providing fun, interactive and entertaining solutions', 12Snap is one of the key players in the European mobile marketing sector. By exploiting the opportunities offered by the development of wireless technology as a new media channel, 12Snap has created personalized and targeted advertising campaigns specializing in the fast-changing youth market.

Apart from wireless marketing 12Snap also provides consumers with a host of interactive entertainment and shopping services which are available through 98 per cent of today's mobile phones. 12Snap currently has 14 million aggregated permission-based opt-in users making contact with millions of consumers each month. Top global brands to have partnered with 12Snap include McDonald's, 20th Century Fox, Emap and Nestlé.

Selecting an agency

For companies looking to use the services of a mobile marketing agency, the factors to consider include:

- *Permission-based campaigns.* Although most mobile marketing agencies now conform to guidelines such as those drawn up by the Mobile Marketing Association, it is still worth making sure that opt-in models are deployed.
- *Track record.* Corporates need to consider whether an agency's track record is suitable for their needs. For instance, a specialist in youth marketing might not be suitable for an insurance firm.
- *Approach.* Many agencies have radically different approaches and beliefs (some might say prejudices). It is important that the agency chosen is open-minded enough to try something new. A strong belief in personalization never goes amiss, either.

- *Technology.* It is necessary to ensure that the agency has the relevant technology for your requirements. As mobile technology evolves and as applications such as SMS and WAP are transformed, this issue becomes ever more complex.

Mobile mentor: Andrew Bud, CEO, mBlox

The anti-chaos theory

You can always spot a real money-making opportunity, because then the industry is ahead of the press. In bubble technologies like WAP, the media enjoy ecstasies of visionary insight while real firms are still heart-rendingly searching for a customer. But when the market rewards creativity and cleverness, the commentators somehow miss the point.

Mobile marketing has displayed just these symptoms. What has been the public topic of 2001/2? Spam! Articles and editorials and features and letters and seminars and laws. Meanwhile, the real industry understood early on that spam was dumb. Circumstance had presented marketeers with the biggest mass media channel in history (70 per cent population penetration), individually targetable, and they were going to annihilate it by alienating consumers with spam?

While the sterile spam debate thrashed on, real mobile marketeers were experimenting with the real issues: how to capture and hold people's attention so that they would accept and even enjoy a brand's blandishments arriving on their phonetop, such an intimate place. The marketeers learnt that this was a real challenge to their creativity: somehow they had to create an entertaining, compelling, personalized experience, a blend of entertainment and marketing.

To earn people's attention, they needed to create a high-quality experience. So they had to target the right content to the right groups of people at the right time. But just those attributes also maximized the value of the channel to the advertisers, so a symbiosis has come into play. The best user experiences are also the most financially valuable. Spam is not just nasty, it's worthless.

Of course, conceiving and designing a fun and appropriate user interaction based on 160 characters of text is very challenging, and is well on its way to being a real profession. When successful, as Full Six's UK hair lotion campaign to teenagers was, it is deeply impressive. Full Six's simple but subtly designed hair tips service achieved 70 per cent sustained participation, solicited consumer pleas for more when it ended, and delivered a 14 per cent increase in product sales directly attributable to the campaign.

Sadly, even the cleverest campaign lapses into farce and chaos if it falls prey to the weaknesses of the SMS system. Timely and focused campaigns don't do too well if the interactions are slow, the messages are late, and if half are never delivered at all – all depressingly common in operators' networks. All that creativity, ambition and investment, let down by the plumbing! Get even small implementation details wrong, and the quality of the user experience suffers so disastrously that the value of the whole campaign is effectively gutted.

Unfortunately, fixing the SMS plumbing and creating a compelling SMS user experience are professions that sometimes get confused. Most mobile marketeers have learnt that do-it-yourself SMS delivery is a recipe for expensive disaster. Conversely, just because someone knows how to make an SMS experience work doesn't mean he or she knows how to create one.

Yet this sometimes happens in the world of SMS marketing, perhaps because the creatives are off doing something else. They have been beguiled by the siren calls of the mobile operators, who dangle their revenue-share morsels at entertainment designers in exchange for their brands and their souls. Why fight to find the unpredictable and risky marketing sponsorship to launch your hot game when you could reverse-bill it in 'partnership' with an operator? Why reach for 100 per cent of the market and retain all the brand value when you could settle for 30–50 per cent market reach and get 65 per cent of the value at lower risk instead?

Free-to-air entertainment models are difficult and frightening things when the marginal cost of an interaction – unlike the Internet – is decidedly non-zero. But they impose a discipline that ruthlessly fells the unsuccessful or the amateurish and rewards the good: a strong entertainment experience – especially a simple one – well targeted and timed, can generate marketing value far greater than any punters would willingly shell out of their own phone bill. And free-to-air has no glass ceiling, awaiting those who fool themselves that consumers' willingness to pay for more and more content is unlimited.

And that's the significance of mobile marketing to content owners and creatives: if you believe in yourselves, it's the best way to extract scaleable value from a concept, addressing the whole market, without the operators taking an unearned slice of the action.

To the mobile marketeer, creative entertainment concepts are oxygen. The high cost of SMS, the non-availability (until recently) of reliable two-way interactions and the heat-seeking instincts of the mobile entertainment professionals have forced the marketeers to create their own school of simple, effective and fun ideas. How mobile marketing will flourish, once SMS reliability improves and the maturing mobile entertainment industry contributes its experience and properties.

And to the SMS plumber like me, mobile marketing presents a wonderful challenge – the need to respond to a whole range of service requirements and price sensitivities: from the huge community-of-interest broadcast, through to the time-critical multi-move individual game play, and always delivered across all networks to a crisp and demanding service level and price.

Some people prefer to watch the ads rather than the programmes on television, because they're slicker and more compelling. People rely on their mobile phones to stave off boredom and loneliness: we can make mobile marketing an equally exciting and welcome instrument in that quest.

Andrew Bud is CEO of mBlox Limited, the UK-based provider of European SMS transmission services, which he co-founded in 1999. He was previously one of the founders of Omnitel, Italy's second mobile operator, and Strategic Marketing Director for Azlan plc. He has a degree in Engineering from Cambridge University and is a Chartered Engineer.

Last word

As mobile marketing is still in its infancy, and as wireless technology continues to develop at breakneck speed, the options open to marketers increase even further. However, rather than get too bogged down in technological detail, you need to concentrate on the requirements of your target audience. Sometimes this means taking a 'lowest common denominator' approach, using the most basic systems in order to cast the widest net. Most of all, it means making sure a campaign can be delivered reliably and that the solution aids, rather than hinders, your marketing.

eleven

The mobile Internet

Of course, mobile marketing is about more than just text messaging. Indeed, in 1999 very few people were predicting that marketing via SMS would take off. At that time, the future of mobile marketing was represented by another three letter acronym: WAP (wireless application protocol). Who would be bothered about boring old text messages when they had access to the wireless Internet? Well, quite a few people as it turned out. As Marco Argenti, CEO of Italian-based DADA.net, states in his contribution to this book, 'text messaging has been and remains the killer application for mobile data'. But this, lest we forget, is the voice of hindsight. A few years ago most marketers who had caught onto the mobile revolution were hard at work building WAP sites.

Their customers meanwhile were hard at work trying to access them. Slow transmission speeds and frequent connection failures meant that many of those who were open-minded enough to give WAP a go were becoming increasingly disillusioned. To be blunt, WAP was starting to look like a bad joke. However, all is by no means lost for the mobile Internet. Although the early WAP hype now seems to have been something of a false start, technological advancements mean that the usability failings previously encountered will, if not disappear altogether, be greatly alleviated. The so-called 'third generation' (3G) of mobile devices will deliver faster and better quality access to the mobile Internet, and marketers will at last be able to realize its full potential.

A rough ride

WAP (wireless application protocol) was heralded as the first major global technology to make the mobile Internet a reality. And it was, although excessively slow download times and frequent connection failure along with many other usability shortcomings started to make people wonder if the wireless Web would be such a great thing anyway.

In 1999, the year WAP was being tweaked for launch in many countries, not a bad word could be found about this technology. Two years later and headlines such as 'The great WAP flop' and 'RIP WAP' were not uncommon in the European technology press. One Summer 2001 survey in the UK was especially telling. The BRMB study found that of the two-thirds of the population who owned a mobile phone, 85 per cent believed they had an SMS texting facility, while only 13 per cent said they had a WAP-enabled phone. Of that small number, only 37 per cent had used the WAP facility within the last month. Therefore most of those who were aware they were using a WAP device still didn't believe the WAP facility was worth using. As Simon Rogers commented in the *Guardian* at around the same time (July 2001), 'Accessing a breaking news service using WAP just doesn't replicate the usefulness of the net and is little more than another incremental improvement on your phone'.

WAP's rough ride has been made even worse by the remarkable, and generally unpredicted, success of SMS. While WAP had been touted as a 'killer app' for wireless devices, the considerably less flashy SMS received little attention. When it suddenly emerged that in many parts of the world there were 10 SMS users for every one WAP user, and that those SMS users were considerably more devoted than their weary WAP counterparts, it inevitably ruffled a few feathers. However, it is fair to say that rumours regarding the death of WAP have been greatly exaggerated as effective WAP applications, including push messaging over GPRS, have finally emerged.

For most marketers, WAP has become something of a no-go area. The *Financial Times* has dubbed WAP marketing 'the least interesting type of wireless marketing'. However, that too may be starting to change as the hitherto frosty public reception of WAP starts to thaw out. Even so, any marketer stepping into the WAP arena needs to be fully aware of the perceived WAP problems.

WAP problems

Given the scale of the difficulties experienced during the first WAP era, you could probably write a whole book on this subject. But anyway, here are the main reasons for WAP's bumpy ride:

- *Incompatibility with non-mobile Internet.* WAP requires Web pages to be rewritten in the Wireless Markup Language. HTML (HyperText Markup Language), which is the standard code for building Web pages, is not WAP-compatible. This contrasts with the Japanese i-Mode which uses Compact HTML (cHTML), which means standard HTML pages can be converted into an i-Mode format very easily.
- *Content.* WAP has suffered from a distinct lack of content mobile users could find useful on a WAP-based wireless Web. Although many companies have experimented with WAP sites, there is still a long way to go before surfing for hours via WAP is a truly valuable experience. Information underload remains a problem.
- *i-Mode.* Unfavourable comparisons to Japanese i-Mode technology have added salt to WAP's wounds.
- *SMS.* WAP has also suffered from components with the more straightforward SMS.
- *Hype.* The initial WAP hype, which reached its hyperbolic peak in 1999–2000, overstated its case. One UK operator's campaign featuring a WAP-enabled surfboard, and many others like it, gave the impression of a mobile Internet 'surfer's paradise'. The protocol clearly couldn't deliver on this promise.
- *Usability.* Jakob Nielsen, ex-Sun Microsystems engineer and 'guru of Web usability' highlighted WAP's 'miserable usability'. In 2000, Nielsen advised businesses to 'skip the current generation of WAP', but believes WAP 2.0 could have real potential.
- *Network restraints.* Slow connections and downloads for the first wave of WAP meant mobile users downloading WAP sites (particularly those with graphics) had a lot of spare time on their hands.
- *Not uniform.* Owing to the fact that HTML was not compatible with WAP, they existed in 'two parallel worlds' as one commentator put it. Furthermore, even in the parallel world, WAP was

not uniform. For instance, European WAP developers used a different standard to their US counterparts.

The WAP Forum

Originating in 1999, WAP's development has been overseen by the WAP Forum (www.wapforum.org), an industry consortium bringing together key players in the mobile industry. Rather than adopt HTML to develop WAP content, developers created a new code specifically for mobile devices. This, most experts agree, was a mistake as it meant an uphill struggle for any content developers wanting to work with WAP. Since 1999, the WAP Forum has worked closely with its Web counterpart, W3C (World Wide Web Consortium). Now the WAP Forum and W3C have agreed on XHTML as their future. The WAP Forum also works closely with the GSM Association.

The WAP brand

To be fair, many of the problems with WAP are not really its fault. After all, WAP is only a protocol, and not a bad one at that. However, the world WAP has extended to encompass the entire mobile Internet experience via WAP-enabled devices. And, up until now, that experience has been patchy to say the least.

As any brand strategist would agree, the success of a product or service depends not simply on its value, but rather its perceived value. So, whatever WAP will be able to offer mobile users in the future, the present negative perception will take a while to erase. Even the WAP evangelists are starting to realize that it suffers from a certain public image problem. For instance, at the start of 2002 the staunchly pro-WAP Web site WAPInsight (www.wapinsight.com) conceded that 'the signs are increasing that WAP as a brand name is dying'. The site reported the demise of the UK chain of retail stores run by MPC Telecom, called TheWAPStore, and said the 'WAP' element of the name sparked off negative associations among the public. GPRS, which has had less brand abuse, may be a more attractive acronym to associate yourself with.

Say WAP?

A broad cross-section of industry comment regarding the present and future state of the mobile Internet:

With fast access speeds and highly capable devices, our services are undergoing a huge evolution. We strive to produce the solutions that our customers demand, and this now is possible. Contemplating the incredible array of content on the Internet today, we are clear about the potential of 3G.

Martin Tufft, Head of Applications and Services, MANX Telecom, UK

The usability of current WAP services is severely reduced because of a misguided use of design principles from traditional Web design. This situation is exactly equivalent to Web design problems in 1994, when sites contained 'brochureware' that followed design principles that worked great in print (say, big images) but didn't work in an interactive medium.

Jakob Nielsen, usability guru and WAP sceptic

WAP phones allow for even easier and more widespread invasions of privacy, opening up the potential for wireless hackers to tap into stored data as well as phone and e-mail communication.

Damon Leigh, urban75.com

I am in love with my short messaging service. The simplest technology that has to do with wireless is my favourite and the most useful. What do I need WAP for? So I can scroll through a bunch of Web sites that I don't look at from my computer to begin with?

Benjamin Silverman, founder of Dotcom Scoop

The W3C regards the Web as a universal space, and device-independence is a critical piece. Recognizing the needs of digital cellular phones and other portable devices, and incorporating those considerations into the development of Web specifications is critical for the Web's success.

Tim Berners Lee, inventor of the World Wide Web and Director of the World Wide Web Consortium (W3C)

Big in Japan

In Japan, the mobile Internet has long been a part of people's everyday lives, thanks to i-Mode technology. Indeed, i-Mode was the first system to put cyberspace in people's pockets with low cost and continuing access. According to figures from cellular operator NTT DoCoMo, most i-Mode subscribers in Japan use their phones primarily for Internet access. This has been the situation since September 2000 when it was revealed that users spent 41 per cent of their phone time using e-mail features (including image exchange) and only 34 per cent of their time making phone calls.

Such has been the tremendous success of i-Mode that one journalist has referred to the comparison between it and WAP as 'a mismatch between a weedy infant and a body building giant'. Even when i-Mode was first launched in February 1999 it was able to offer a very user-friendly and affordable mobile Internet. However, it should be noted that WAP and i-Mode are not entirely incompatible. Indeed, in Hong Kong Orange set up a WAP service that enables subscribers to access i-Mode content. It is possible, in theory at least, to convert cHTML (the Web building code used by i-Mode) so that it can be viewed on WAP phones. That said, i-Mode is much more compatible with the fixed Internet than WAP, which requires Web site owners to completely redevelop their standard site.

Pioneered as always by teens, i-Mode has become popular with all ages in Japan. Owing to its phenomenal success at home, world domination could now be on the cards. In 2001, the stop-start progress of 3G caused NTT DoCoMo to explore the European potential for i-Mode. Initially the plan was to launch i-Mode across Europe before March 2002, but technological setbacks (namely the slow rollout of GPRS services and incompatibility with some European systems) meant that this launch had to be postponed indefinitely.

However, NTT DoCoMo is working with Dutch operator KPN Mobiel and has made inroads into the German market. At the time of writing, no formal statement has been made regarding i-Mode and the UK. In November 2001 NTT DoCoMo CEO Keiji Tachilkawa was reported to say (in the German business paper *Handelsblatt*) that 'we're most interested in the markets of France,

Italy and Spain'. The company has also announced their launch of 3G mobile systems, considered a potential threat to i-Mode's success outside Japan.

GPRS and 3G

GPRS and 3G technologies (both of which are discussed in more detail in 'Future technologies', Chapter 12) will lead to a faster more powerful and cost-effective mobile Internet. However, there is still debate as to whether they will replace WAP or simply improve it. Certainly, GPRS is presently giving WAP a much-needed makeover.

Mobile Internet marketing principles

Owing to the early shortcomings of WAP, many remain deeply sceptical about the potential of the mobile Internet. However, for those marketers with the time, money and resources to invest in their mobile marketing activity, mobile Internet services can work in conjunction with text messaging to capitalize on the full power of the mobile medium. After all, there are WAP users out there. No, seriously. There are. The numbers may be dwarfed by those for text messaging, but they are still significant. The emergence of GPRS networks mean that the mobile Internet is not only a reality, but quite an attractive one at that. If you are interested in offering a WAP/GPRS service, you need to be sure the technology will not disappoint mobile users. That is not to say WAP services cannot work. They can, but you will need to understand the difference between WAP and the standard Web:

● *Boil your service down.* 'Lavish design may work on the Web if users have a big screen PC, but on a small-screen device, designers must boil each service down to its essence and show much less information,' advises Jakob Nielsen, who conducted a WAP usability study in late 2000. Minimalism may be back out of fashion, but it is essential in order to win over WAP users.

- *Make sure your content is relevant.* Directory services, such as the WAP version of Yell.com, have already proved attractive to WAP users.
- *Think of the capabilities of a mobile device.* In some ways, WAP is limited in comparison to the standard Internet. However, there are also benefits, such as the ability to call a number directly from a WAP site (see Yell.com case study).
- *Test for usability.* In order to minimize any technical hitches, any WAP service should be tested prior to launch for usability failings. These failings could include poor navigation, slow download times or a cluttered layout.
- *Tailor your service.* Many usability problems arise from the different specifications of individual handsets.
- *Provide real-time information.* One of the attractions of WAP for users is access to live information when they are away from home or the office. For instance, finance site ADVFN.com offers real-time trading information via WAP devices.
- *Keep track of market attitudes.* More than in any other area of mobile marketing, future attitudes towards WAP remain unpredictable. Instead of concentrating solely on technological improvements, it is advisable to focus on how customers are using WAP devices.
- *Place fun before commerce.* As Nikesh Arora explains below, the secret to making WAP work is to make sure commerce follows entertainment.

Mobile mentor: Nikesh Arora, Board Member, T-Mobile International

M-fun before m-commerce: making WAP work

There's been no shortage of hype surrounding WAP mobile technology, with the industry pushing the notion of surfing the World Wide Web on a handset which clearly left consumers disappointed. With an initial focus purely on technology marketing, the handsets made it difficult for consumers to perceive the real benefit of mobile online services.

However there is a growing confidence as consumers are increasingly using mobile online services for simple, context relevant bits of information like checking sports scores, e-mail, chatting and dating and listening to music clips.

There are a number of key product principles for busting through the hype and getting consumers to see what WAP can really offer. The key is to deliver a killer consumer experience by focusing on delivering a quality product.

- Make it easy. Reconfiguring phone settings and entering log-ins and passwords does not encourage easy adoption or return users.
- Make it relevant. Quick bits of information that are easy to access and understand.
- Make it trustworthy. It has to work the same way each and every time.
- Make it entertaining. History has shown that it is entertainment not commerce that is the key driver of technology in the mass market.

For example, the Internet was born as a mechanism for information sharing, but practically since its inception, 'sex' has been the most searched for word by users online. What is it finally replaced by? MP3. Digital television was driven by sports, and while e-mail has revolutionized the way businesses communicate, the mechanism has also become synonymous with the distribution of jokes, pictures and chain letters.

Mobile online services are no different, and clearly entertainment will drive mass-market acceptance. This has already been proven with the success of i-Mode in Japan, where the most popular services include such simple ideas as ringtones and icons. The T-Mobile experience is proving to follow a similar trend, where top services include sports scores, chatting and dating and sending music clips to friends.

Commerce has a place in the mobile world but regardless of how fast the technology moves, it won't take off until the market is ready. Consumers must first learn to depend on these services before they will trust the device with their financial details. Right now the industry must learn to provide end-to-end solutions which centre on entertaining, topical services in order to drive mass market acceptance.

Nikesh Arora is a board member of T-Mobile International and heads up the new business area internationally.

Case study: Yell.com's WAP service

Directories, such as Yell.com's WAP site, have proved to be a modest success among the small but growing army of WAP users. Indeed, while some companies have abandoned their WAP activity, Yell.com invested in improving their service at the start of 2002.

The service, which aims to offer users easier access to the Yell.com database of classified listings (nearly 2 million UK businesses) now offers additional features. Some of these improvements indicate the potential advantages of the mobile Internet over the desktop Web experience. For instance, it includes a 'call the number' feature, enabling users to phone a specific company directly. The improved service also personalized the search facility to individual handsets. This means users can narrow searches to business type, company name and location. 'The format of the previous site and its delivery was not compatible with all handsets,' said Nick Gray, marketing executive at Smart 421, the technology group which developed the service for Yell.com. 'The way the new site has been built means that it recognizes which handset is being used and delivers content for it.' These enhancements were the result of customer research, which involved compiling data from Talking Pages to find out more about caller habits.

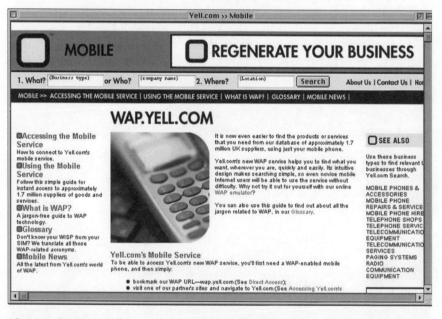

Figure 11.1 Yell's WAP guide indicates the potential for the mobile Internet

Case study: location-based WAP marketing

UK high street retailers HMV, Lush, Oddbins and Superdrug have implemented mobile marketing campaigns using Brainstorm's UK-wide location-based WAP service. With the exception of Superdrug, who ran the service in their top 150 stores, the retailers use the service in all stores in the UK and Northern Ireland to notify potential customers of special deals.

Initially, these offers were available exclusively to the 2 million users of BT Genie and other WAP services. These consumers had the ability to receive details of over 30,000 location-based shopping offers covering on average 1,200 individual store locations across the UK via Brainstorm's shopping service. The Promotion Finder is highly location sensitive, working to within 500 metres of a user's geographical location. Within the London area alone, the service offers the capability to drill down to 100 different regions of London including specific parts of the West End.

'HMV is very interested in understanding how effective pull-based mobile marketing like the WAP Promotion Finder is across a wide audience group,' says John Wheatley, Business Development Manager at HMV UK. 'I think there's a lot more to mobile marketing than just SMS marketing alerts, and we'll be looking at 3G platforms as soon as they're ready.'

Figure 11.2   Brainstorm helps companies offer location-based services

Reasons to be cheerful

Although WAP has not had it easy so far, there are reasons to be (cautiously) optimistic about the future of the mobile Internet, WAP and GPRS. Here are some of them:

- *XHTML*. Released in early 2000, this advanced Web-building 'language' merges aspects of WAP and the Web, enabling companies to create a single, extensible interface that can be adapted to multiple types of fixed and mobile browsers. In plain English, XHTML offers a bridge between WAP and the Web. Nokia hopes to incorporate an XHTML-based browser into all its phones in the future. Motorola, Ericsson and Siemens are also planning to incorporate XHTML as the 'backbone' of future services.
- *Open standard*. WAP is an open standard. In other words it is not owned by any one business or organization. This means anyone can adopt the standard and pursue its development. I-Mode, in contrast, is a proprietary standard owned by NTT DoCoMo.
- *Global prominence*. WAP is about as global as a mobile technology can get, with stronger US awareness than SMS.
- *GPRS*. Before 3G makes a real impact on how people use mobile technology, we have GPRS (general packet radio service). Although it may not be able to offer as much as 3G, it is already changing the mobile Internet experience for the better. Also, WAP works with, not against, GPRS because it has been designed to be as independent as possible from the underlying network technology.
- *The pendulum effect*. The WAP backlash has almost been as hysterical as the hype that surrounded its birth. However, as the media coverage has become more negative, the number of people in Europe and the United States accessing the mobile Internet has steadily risen. In line with the pendulum effect which always surrounds once-hyped Internet technologies, the buzz should swing back in favour of the mobile Internet.

RIP SMS?

Some people equate the rise of the mobile Internet with the demise of SMS text messaging. Why would anyone want to hang on to this rather basic technology when the whole shiny future of the mobile Internet awaits? The people who tend to ponder this question are those who were rather surprised, and maybe a little disgruntled, when SMS became so popular in the first place. Not since Beatlemania has a youth phenomenon become so huge, so quickly, and managed to gain such mainstream appeal.

However, SMS has almost grown too fast. Many fear that its rapid rise indicates that it could have an equally hasty end once the mobile Internet starts to take hold of the collective imagination. This argument is weak for a number of reasons. Firstly, the technological advancements which are making a user-friendly mobile Internet a reality are also leading to improvements in text messaging. SMS-based services offered over GPRS or '2.5G' networks are able to deliver faster response times, longer messages and enable multi-media content to be sent.

Rather than signalling the end for text messaging, third generation and GPRS will help it to evolve. Just as cinema has survived the threat of television, video and DVD, so too will the unique benefits of text messaging ensure its longevity. Of course, it is unlikely that the term SMS will have an equally long shelf life. Already EMS (enhanced messaging service) and MMS (multimedia messaging service) are gaining popular currency, as people are getting used to the next evolutionary stage for the text message.

Last word

Whether WAP remains a taboo three-letter word or not, the mobile Internet has a positive future. Indeed, in some parts of the globe it has a positive present. In Japan, the Internet has become the main reason people use their mobile devices. Currently, there are two things preventing the mobile Internet from realizing its maximum potential elsewhere: user experience and user acceptance. As user experience improves, so should more people accept what the mobile Internet has to offer. For those marketers entering into this mobilized information space, it is important to keep an eye on how people are using the technology, and understand the fixed mobile Internet difference. It may not yet, or ever, be a surfer's paradise, but the mobile Internet's waters are warming all the time.

twelve

Future technologies

In the early days of the mobile phone, its uses were limited. In fact, for about a decade voice calls remained the only possibility. Now, however, it is hard to find something a mobile phone can't do. Text messaging, mobile shopping, Web browsing and mobile gaming were just the start. Phones can now include built-in MP3 players, FM radios, digital cameras and professional digital voice recorders. Some can also be used as a handheld computer or PDA (personal digital assistant). Voice-activation and the ability to send photos and even video via mobile devices have also proved to be a possibility. One phone, the Samsung A400, which is available in Asia, even enables women to monitor their ovulation as it can tell when their most fertile days are. So now phones can not only help users communicate, they can even help them get pregnant.

This chapter, with informative contributions from mobile technology experts Chris Hayward and Mike Short, looks at some of the developments which are helping this shift from monofunctional mobile phone to multifunctional mobile device. I should also point out that all the technologies mentioned in this chapter are only future technologies in the sense that their potential is yet to be fully realized.

3G

3G, standing for third generation, has long been heralded as the nirvana of mobile technology. While the first generation of mobile devices were limited to voice calls, second generation (2G) devices offered more. Indeed, 2G made possible SMS, WAP and mobile shopping. 3G, however, goes a whole lot further. What 3G offers is far more powerful data transmission across mobile networks. Whereas the intermediary 2.5G devices offer transmission rates of up to 384 kilobits per second, 3G's transmission speed is five times faster, averaging about two megabits per second.

So what does all this increased bandwidth actually mean? If the mobile operators are to be believed, it means less hassle for the mobile user. Problems of slow message speeds, congested mobile traffic and stop-start Internet access should all but disappear with 3G devices. Furthermore, 3G brings with it the possibility of mobile television and enables people to participate in a videoconference, send vivid pictures and listen to audiofiles.

However, while 3G looks set to improve mobile devices, it will not fundamentally change the way people use mobile devices. In a January 2002 interview with *Business World*, Carl Sandelin, the Senior Vice-President for Marketing at Nokia Networks in the Philippines, said that people should not be intimidated by 3G. 'The important thing is evolution and not revolution,' he said. 'It does not remove existing services but enhances them with more bandwidth. These services drive evolution.'

Although 3G is eventually expected everywhere, it has not had a smooth ride. In Europe, telecommunications firms spent enormous amounts on frequencies alone and consequently were left with limited resources with which to develop the network and infrastructure. As a result, 3G had been in the pipeline (literally) for years before it was announced that 2002 would be the European launch date. Some developed countries in Asia, such as Singapore, are expecting 3G to arrive later, in 2004 or 2005. However, the networks will be in place before compatible devices hit the high street.

As telecommunications companies have had to bid for the limited 3G frequencies at the outset, it means that they have to weigh the long-term benefit against mid-term cost very carefully, especially when investors are demanding a relatively speedy return on investment. There has even been speculation that 3G may take even longer to reach Asia (and longer still for the United States), owing to the expensive auction process. Even in Europe, conservative estimates state that it will not be until 2007/8 before 3G penetration has reached the levels of GSM (the current standard).

Mobile mentor: Chris Hayward, CEO, Textploitation Ltd

Notes on the third generation

When I was a young lad, one of the predictions of science fiction that particularly thrilled me was the idea that in 2001 we'd all be walking around with electronic gadgets in our pockets giving access to all the information held on any computer system in the world at an instant. Just like we'd all take our holidays on the moon. But actually this is one forecast that has pretty much come true now, since around 600 million of us have just such a device. The problem is, we don't all realize it because, for historical reasons, we happen to call the thing a 'telephone'.

The fact that most of us limit our use of the mobile to voice communication leads to some pretty nonsensical situations. One example. You want to check your bank or credit card account while on the move. You use your GSM phone to ring a call centre, talk to an operator, give answers to their security questions and wait while they type your details into their computer terminal and read out the answer to you. And all of this using a digital device which is quite capable of data communications direct to the same computer system, thus saving you and your bank a whole load of time, hassle and money.

Of course, there have been various attempts to sort this out and provide proper mobile data access. I'd say we've seen two generations to date. The first generation had the mobile phone acting as a modem, with no user terminal functionality. Great for power business users to connect up their laptop, lousy for most of us for whom one mobile device is quite enough to carry around with us. The second generation was WAP – a valiant attempt to put user terminal functionality into the handset. But by applying the Internet browser model, which was designed for big screens and fast data links, to the constrained limits of the mobile handset, a great opportunity was missed.

What I see as the third generation is the (belated) realization that there's a lot you can do with the infrastructure and terminal devices in use today. SMS provides a bearer network which can support a user interaction of reasonable complexity, using character input and limited menu options. OK, it might seem a little clunky for those brought up on Wintel bloatware and graphic interfaces. But the truth is that good, tight transaction processing, coupled with intelligent interface design – and a little imagination – can deliver serious business and customer benefits – even when dealing with low resolution screen display, limited keypad interaction and transmission delays between key entries. After all, we put men on the moon without the aid of Windows!

Obviously the interface is going to get better in the coming years, as MMS, high resolution colour screens, and even 3G kick in. But we need to be building models today using plain old SMS. These can then be adapted and improved as these technologies become mainstream. Perhaps the key challenge for now is to convince 600 million users that the thing in their pockets is not a phone at all, but actually their personal data gateway to a world of information.

Chris Hayward is CEO of Textploitation Ltd, a wireless applications company specializing in the use of SMS to deliver high value interactive propositions and consumer products. Chris managed the launch of Virgin Mobile, the world's first virtual network operator, and managed the trial of BT Cellnet/Barclaycard Visacash project, which saw the first download of e-cash over a GSM network onto an e-purse smart card. He is also author of the Reuters Business Insight report on m-commerce and is an Executive Board Member of the Global Mobile Commerce Forum.

Case study: Nokia's 3G survey

A 2001 study undertaken by the HPI Research Group on behalf of Nokia highlighted the potential for the mobile entertainment services in third generation mobile devices. The study demonstrated that the core mobile-phone market (16–45 year olds) was excited by the pace of technological changes, which they expected would make life more fun and stimulating.

For the study, HPI interviewed over 3,300 people in 11 key global markets across three continents. Those interviewed consisted of the core target market for the 3G offering, namely teenagers, young adults and family adults, all of whom currently have mobile phones for personal use. The markets were Brazil, Denmark, Germany, Italy, Japan, Korea, Singapore, Spain, Sweden, the United Kingdom and the United States. Although conducted in June 2001, the study still provides an insight into what end users want from their mobile devices, especially as the study was based on future technologies.

Study participants were asked both about 3G handsets and in which 3G features and services they would be interested. In all, consumers were presented with over 30 prospective features and questioned regarding their interest in the features. Consumers stated that they would want, on average, 14 features, clearly suggesting that the 3G handset will be seen as multi-functional. Easily the most popular feature with 81 per cent was SMS texting, probably as this was already available to the consumer, and thus more tangible. Following this, texting, audio/visual and information services were particularly prominent.

When categorized into three separate 3G service areas of messaging/photo, entertainment and information, it was clear that the 3G handset was also seen as an entertainment device. In particular, 72 per cent of respondents stated they would like to have at least one entertainment service available on their 3G terminal. Among the younger respondents, enthusiasm was even greater, with 9 out of 10 'definitely' wanting at least one of the entertainment features. The top five entertainment services attractive to respondents were:

● listening to radio;
● requesting single songs;
● requesting albums;
● watching live television;
● playing games, alone and interactively.

Interestingly, the respondents did not see the handset as a direct replacement for other electronic devices, but rather as a multi-functional device that can be used for entertainment when they do not have access to a television, video or game machine. For example, three-quarters of consumers indicated they would use the 3G features when travelling or outside the home.

Respondents were shown a video of how 3G might be used in the future, as well as photos of how a 3G handset might look. Following this, over 90 per cent of this core market stated that they were excited about the developments in mobile telephony, with over half expressing they 'were very excited'. In fact, just 4 per cent of the core market stated that they would not be interested in purchasing one. The US and Asian markets were most enthusiastic, with Germany, Spain and the UK slightly less enthused.

MMS: 'SMS on steroids'

Third generation and other technological advances will not mean the death of text messaging, but they will mean the full evolution from SMS to MMS. MMS, or the multimedia messaging service, has been nicknamed 'SMS on steroids' owing to its advanced and more powerful capabilities. While these advancements began with EMS (enhanced messaging services), MMS goes further. MMS, which uses 3G technology, enables messages to incorporate multimedia elements (photos, audio, video). In addition, the 160 character limit no longer needs to apply.

On MMS devices, ringtones will also be radically transformed. Instead of just annoying bleeps, there will be different instrument settings which could make the term 'musical ringtone' mean just that. From a marketer's perspective, MMS will provide more innovative ways to reach mobile users, and the visual elements will enable marketers to create a more unified brand identity (by matching the look of their Web site, products etc). MMS has been described as a hybrid of e-mail and SMS, taking the best of both systems. It will certainly help to bridge the gap between text messaging and the mobile Internet. For instance, e-mail addresses as well as mobile phone numbers can be used when creating an MMS message. However, as 3G is not going to reach GSM levels for some years to come, SMS is not going anywhere fast.

Nokia was one of the first of the big mobile firms to treat MMS seriously, unveiling its first MMS phone, the 7650, in Barcelona in November 2001. The phone, launched in Europe in Spring 2002, was billed by Nokia as being the start of the move away from 'hear what I say' to 'see what I mean' devices. The phone included a digital camera, and the images it creates can either be displayed on its colour screen or sent over the GPRS (General Packet Radio Service) mobile network. The company also expects that MMS will be standard across the Nokia range by the middle of 2003.

One thing worth remembering, however, is that flashy graphics do not determine the success of a marketing campaign. That is to say, even when you are able to incorporate video or dynamic images within your marketing messages, it does not mean that you should.

As the lesson of the fixed Internet has taught us, consumers want value, not state-of-the-art gimmickry. There is certainly no denying that some of the most spectacular dot.com disasters – of which Boo.com is the prime example – were also the best looking. As Web users want to absorb information on a Web page in as short a time as possible, most Web developers now shun 'whistles and bells' in favour of a more stripped-down approach. It is also true that many of the most successful e-mail newsletters – such as the *New York*

Times' Today's headline' – are formatted in plain text, not HTML. After all, it is unlikely that either the home PC or the mobile phone is ever going to be able to create the same visual environment as, say, a cinema. So instead of trying to create the most visually exciting (and most expensive) campaigns, marketers must not be dazzled by technology and should concentrate on what consumers want and are prepared to use.

Figure 12.1   MMS phones increase the potential for marketing messages

---

Mobile mentor: Mike Short, Chairman of the Mobile Data Association

Go 4 it

Mobile data capabilities will be made available soon with new technologies such as colour screens and larger displays, high speed and packet data (faster network speeds); multimedia messaging (MMS); instant messaging (connecting to Internet personalization and buddy lists); location and m-commerce applications; numbering and addressing schemes.

Multimedia messaging and 3G will add more capability, to help us move from the verbal to the visual world of screen graphics and imagery. This should really support much more customer permission based marketing, and customer relationship management (CRM). Many partnerships will also emerge to grow SMS for banking, advertising, sponsorship, interactive media (music, television and newspapers), premium rate services, games and gambling. These in turn will add to the current information, news, weather and events already personalized and sent via text and graphics in the modern messaging world. However, they will also encourage new forms of communications, new value chains, as well as many new trade or wholesale partnerships.

Mobile marketing may have been absent in the early years of texting, but the opportunities now continue to multiply with new messaging technology and value chain enablers. Also, more personalization will be added to maximize relevance and to make the best use of the capabilities of mobile.

Mike Short is the Chairman of the Mobile Data Association and Vice President of mmO2.

Interactive voice response

Interactive voice response (IVR) is not, strictly speaking, a future technology. In the context of this book, it is practically prehistoric. Indeed, IVR predated the Web, let alone WAP. However, as the popularity of mobile communications continues to avalanche, IVR is back on the marketer's menu. IVR enables phone users to access voice-based information by dialling a number, listening to prompts, and entering responses into the keypad. It is increasingly used in conjunction with SMS, and often helps to collect necessary subscriber information at the start of a campaign. IVR has also been used with e-mail, enabling users to call in and listen to e-mails by text-to-speech.

Bluetooth

Bluetooth, a technology that has been in development since the 1990s, was originally intended to be a cable replacement technology, for instance enabling a simple connection between a computer and a printer. Now, however, the Bluetooth vision has become considerably bigger, opening up a new world of wireless connectivity. Through a Bluetooth-enabled device, a 'personal network' is created around the user. 'In addition to the obvious benefits of synchronizing calendars between a PDA, mobile phone and notebook PC, the benefits of a personal network, which travels with you, are almost limitless,' says Simon Ellis, Marketing Chairman of Ericsson's Bluetooth Special Internet Group. 'By simply walking down a road you can easily join and quit dozens of ad hoc networks in streets and buildings, checking for information of personal interest to you, such as information on specific goods while passing through a shopping centre.'

Other commentators such as Claudia Aranger, Manager of the Wireless Initiative at Deloitte Consulting, have been equally enthusiastic. Aranger has claimed that the technology could solve the connectivity and compatibility issues we presently experience. 'Once it's implemented widely, you won't have to sit and program something into every machine you use to make sure other machines can read them,' she has said.

If Bluetooth were to take off in the way its developers hope it will, all PCs would become replaced by wireless devices. However, this is a very big if. Although Bluetooth is predicted to become a standard feature in notebook PCs by 2005, very few Bluetooth products actually exist. Even when they are developed, the challenge will be to make sure that different products work well together. And so the Bluetooth fantasy – where everyday items such as a fridge can communicate with your mobile devices (and tell you, for instance, when you have run out of milk) – remains in the realm of science fiction.

Bluetooth, like WAP, has also been criticized as being a technology for technology's sake. As the market remains uninterested, the largest obstacle is perhaps the lack of consumer knowledge. As Ovum analyst Rob Gear has put it, 'Bluetooth has to be everywhere for it to be any good'. Security and the high cost of Bluetooth chips are two further hurdles to be overcome.

XHTML

XHTML, standing for Extensible HyperText Markup Language, is a more advanced and flexible form of the Web-building code HTML.

As such it has the potential to fill the gap between the development of sites for WAP and sites for the standard Web. Previously, Web builders wanting to move onto the mobile Internet needed to completely rewrite their sites. XHTML theoretically enables the integration of content from various platforms.

Nokia, Motorola, Ericsson and Siemens have all expressed their enthusiasm for this Web standard. 'With XHTML, we now have a unique opportunity to start creating and implementing visually appealing, yet backward WAP-compatible services that will satisfy the requirements of the future as well as ensure a smooth evolution path for current services,' says Anssi Vanjoki, Nokia's Executive Vice President.

According to other experts, XHTML will enable the entire power of the Web to be unleashed. Ultimately, says Accenture's Richard Siber, 'XHTML begins to eliminate the challenges that the burgeoning mobile data industry has experienced to date'.

Mobile manufacturers, operators and software developers have all made moves to incorporate XHTML into the heart of future mobile services. Nokia, never one to shy away from future technologies, has been the first to release a demo version of an XHTML-based browser for mobile devices.

GPRS: giving the mobile Internet a facelift

Although not as advanced as 3G technology, GPRS (General Packet Radio Service) is the interim technology heralded by many as the saviour of the wireless Web. It is an enhancement to the GSM mobile communication system that supports data packets. GPRS enables the continuous flow of Internet data packets over the mobile communication system for such applications as Web browsing and file transfer, and GPRS phones have the capacity to transit data at speeds of up to 144 kilobits per second.

Because it is based on packet switching rather than circuit technology, GPRS means WAP can be charged on a data throughput rather than time basis. Furthermore, it will lead to always-on access rather than having to be accessed through the dialling up of a service. What this all means, in theory at least, is an enhanced mobile Internet experience a world away from the problems associated with WAP in the early days. One of the advantages of GPRS is that it enables 24-hour Internet access, but people only pay for the hours they use. The first wave of GPRS phones included the Siemens ME45 and the Ericsson T39, and more are on their way. Vizzavi was the first UK mobile content provider to launch content tailored for GPRS handsets. WAP games Chess and Pass It On have been developed to exploit the higher speed and always-on connectivity of GPRS networks. However, GPRS is not seen as an end in itself but rather as the stepping stone between 2G and 3G.

As Marco Argenti discusses below, GPRS also enables picture messaging which he believes could be the next 'killer' mobile application.

Mobile mentor: Marco Argenti, Managing Director, DADA.net

Picture messaging: the next killer app?

Text messaging has been and remains the killer application for mobile data. With over 30 billion messages exchanged every month worldwide, it defies e-mail as the most widespread means of digital communication. Next to text messaging, logos and ringtones are definitely the most popular consumer application on mobile phones. For people living in North America, it's hard to believe how popular this form of low-end multimedia messaging is until they travel to Europe or some parts of Asia, and listen to any sort of tunes come out of ringing phones.

The ringtones and logos phenomenon, once a privilege for Nokia users, is now available to owners of several other brands that support the so-called EMS, or enhanced messaging service. In the evolutionary path from text messaging to logos/ringtones, EMS and then MMS, which promises to give true multimedia messaging capabilities to mobile devices, one may wonder what will be the killer app that drives adoption for these new standards, and that ultimately drives people to upgrade their handsets.

Undoubtedly ringtones will remain strong, especially when, with MMS, they will become much more pleasant-sounding by adding polyphony and different instrument settings. Picture messaging is a different thing: here we need to differentiate between 'screen graphics', ie anything that is ornamental to the phone, such as a logo, a wallpaper, screensaver etc, and 'picture messaging' in the strictest sense, where the picture itself is at the heart of communication. Then the question is: would people like to receive pictures on their phones? Probably. Would people like to send pictures from *their* or their friends' phones? I think definitely so.

There is nothing new in exchanging bitmaps of course; anybody can do it through a PC. But how many pictures do we receive through e-mail? Not many. This is simply because the process of going from an image, either analog or digital, to an e-mail message is still cumbersome at best. Once phones are equipped with cameras, then everything will change, provided that the process for taking and sending a picture over a wireless link is an easy one. Nokia has announced a phone, the 7650, that promises just that: point, click, select an entry from the address book, send to an e-mail address. It's that easy. The phone works over existing GPRS or 2.5G networks, so connection time, and cost, are likely not to be concerns. Now that changes everything, doesn't it? I believe this is the first instance of photography truly becoming portable. I can imagine hundreds of scenarios in which people on the move may want to share moments, places, emotions, events, instantly with their friends, families, co-workers. Mind you, this is not videoconferencing. This is mobile photography: in fact, the micro-camera lens in the Nokia phone is not pointing at the user's face, but it's at the back of the phone, pointing outwards, like a camera. Imagine also the applications in a business environment, ranging from real estate to insurance to surveillance and so on.

As always, the popularity of this form of communication will be dependent on the ease of use, the cost of the service and, most importantly, the carriers' open-mindedness to let people exchange messages across different networks. In other words, it is for the carriers to win – if they see the opportunity coming and try facilitating adoption – or pass on what could be the next biggest money-maker after SMS – if they decide to impose usage limitations or high prices for the service.

At present Mario Argenti is one of the 50 members of the Commerce Partner Advisory Board of Microsoft. Managing Director of Wireless Solutions (a company controlled by DADA), Argenti, as a Managing Director, is responsible for DADA's wireless activities.

Figure 12.2   Multimedia handsets are growing in popularity

The SMS 'training ground'

SMS, viewed by many as the simplest and most straightforward mobile technology, has been dubbed a 'training ground' that will help pave the way for 3G services. For instance, mobile users will get used to the idea of paying 'per item' SMS charges, and this will give operators less of an uphill struggle when they roll out their 3G services.

In terms of marketing, SMS has a further role to play for 3G. By building branded services for SMS, marketers and content owners can lay the foundations for their 3G activity, when they carry their services over. Ann Lynch, co-director of Wireless Internet Services at Probe Research has called SMS advertising a 'perfect interim solution'. However, although it is true that the incredible popularity of SMS will ultimately help to create a 3G-friendly environment for operators, marketers and consumers, it is wrong to assume that this is SMS's only long-term value. Many believe (myself included) that it is equally wrong to assume that all consumers will automatically and immediately switch from short, text-based messages to audiovisuals or wireless Internet equivalents. Some will, for sure, but the period of overlap could be longer than has been predicted.

Future phones

Technological advances have helped to turn the humble mobile phone into an entertainment console. In 2001, Nokia launched a phone that stretched the definition to new limits, as it doubled as a radio and an MP3 player. Other possibilities for future phones include:

● *Television.* Mobile television will be a logical extension to the 3G phone's capabilities.
● *Picture messaging.* 'Once phones are equipped with cameras, then everything will change,' explains Marco Argenti in his 'mobile mentor' slot.

- *Bar code readers.* Bar code readers will facilitate m-payment, and could be included in every phone.
- *Instant messenger.* Instant messenger applications may be fully integrated with mobile technology.

Last word

Of course, any predictions regarding the future of mobile usage are likely to get it at least slightly incorrect. After all, very little was said about SMS until it emerged how popular the technology was proving. One thing, however, is certain. End users, not technologists, shape the market. Consequently, marketers need to stay abreast not only of technological developments, but also of the way people respond to them.

Postscript: the mobile marketer's survival guide

Drawing on some of the principles discussed elsewhere in this book (and some which aren't), here are 100 ways to increase your mobile marketing shelf life:

1. *Gain permission.* Sending spam will kill your campaign in its tracks.
2. *Think context.* Content is only king if it is placed in the right context.
3. *Add value.* In order to activate mobile users into subscribing to your service you need to add real value. 'This can take the form of entertainment or exclusive access to goods and information,' says 12Snap's MD Anne de Kerckhove.
4. *Interact.* Mobile marketing is not something you do to people, but with them. Engage in two-way interaction and listen to what your subscribers have to say.
5. *Be courageous.* Embracing a new technology takes courage, but as Peter Drucker famously put it, 'Whenever you see a successful business, someone once made a courageous decision'.
6. *Don't follow technology, follow people.* Courage is good, but it

doesn't mean you should take high risks on technology which is yet to prove itself. Follow the way people are actually using technology, not how they could be using it.

7. *Narrowcast messages.* A one size fits all approach will not work in the mobile medium. Marketers must narrowcast, not broadcast messages to assure relevancy for each mobile user.

8. *Monitor campaigns.* The possibilities of downloadable 'agents' or scripts means advertisers will soon be able to track the behavioural patterns of customers even more effectively than they can at present. For instance, it will be possible to tell which ad triggered a purchase, as well as when and with whom the recipient shared the ad with.

9. *Use the right language.* Text messages often communicate in shorthand as a result of the 160 character limit. It is therefore important marketers understand the way people use the medium before making contact.

10. *Be understood.* If you are using acronyms and abbreviations make sure your recipients understand them. While 'U' (for 'you') and 'gr8' (for 'great') are commonplace, some acronyms used in 'text dictionaries' will confuse most users. Furthermore, says Aerodeon's Andrew Jones, 'this language evolves – a fact which is frequently overlooked'.

11. *Join the tribe.* Andrew Jones, among others, has associated the rise of text messaging with a growth in what the marketing academics like to call 'neo-tribalism'. These 'tribes', linked by networking technologies, have their own patterns and rules. This is especially true in the youth market, where any misjudged marketing message risks ridicule from other members of the tribe. Language plays a key part in becoming accepted. Ideally, though, marketers not only want to join a tribe but lead it.

12. *Don't oversell.* People do not buy a mobile phone to receive blatant advertising. Think from the outside in and try to grasp what target mobile users really want to be sent.

13. *Respect the power of the medium.* The greater the power, the more dangerous the abuse. Permission is essential, but it does not give you a blank cheque. Sending too many messages can be as frustrating to mobile users as sending them uninvited.

14. *Integrate campaigns.* The true power of mobile marketing can be appreciated when it is used with other media. Text messaging can be used to activate an otherwise passive media

campaign. In particular, the Web can be used to provide more detailed information than that conveyed in an SMS message. Furthermore, adding a text message response mechanism to other forms of advertising can help to make traditional media more measurable and accountable.

15. *Encourage a response.* 'Given that mobile marketing facilitates real-time response to marketing messages, brand managers can gain rapid feedback on the effectiveness of their marketing messages across various mediums,' says Carbon Partners' Co-Founder John Farmer.

16. *Differentiate or die.* As the number of commercial text messages rises, differentiation becomes ever more important. Many consumers have reached the point where they are suffering from what Seth Godin (author of *Permission Marketing*) refers to as an 'attention crisis'. In order to capture the imagination of mobile users, make sure your messages offer something genuinely different.

17. *Think laterally.* 'Marketing is not just about pushing ads out to an audience. Anything that gives you a competitive advantage over competitors is good marketing,' explains Mark Mulhern, Executive Director of Wireless Marketing agency Rtn2Sndr.

18. *Be useful.* Generally speaking, campaigns providing useful information prove the most successful, at least from the end user's perspective. The Tubehell SMS service is a prime example. Appointment reminders (for doctors, hairdressers, beauty salons and so on) are another. Think if there is information that you have that mobile users could benefit from receiving.

19. *Concede control.* To embrace mobile marketing you must concede control to your subscribers. The mobile users are the masters of this medium. The only thing you have full control over is the nature of the service you offer. Even then, however, mobile users should be able to provide input and influence.

20. *Make sure you deliver.* For instance, if you are offering an 'exclusive news' service, make sure not to confuse 'exclusivity' with the fact that no one else is interested. If you offer the world, you must deliver it. And with a red ribbon wrapped around it, too. Of course, this has always been important, but when it comes to a medium as personal as the mobile phone, it has even greater significance.

21. *Help users communicate.* Marketers must try to equate the marketing use of text messaging with its prime social use: interaction. The mobile phone, despite being currently made over into a 'personal entertainment console', is still a device which helps people communicate with each other. If you can facilitate this in any way, like Friendsreunited.co.uk managed to do with users of the fixed Internet, the value of your service will increase immensely.

22. *Be human.* Although they may have a common interest, you must remember that no two mobile users are the same. As *The Cluetrain Manifesto* tells us, 'Markets consist of human beings, not demographic sectors'.

23. *Make it viral.* The viral marketing potential of mobile technology exceeds even that of the fixed Internet. If recipients spread your message among their friends, the potential for your campaign will be multiplied as the network effect takes hold.

24. *Surprise recipients.* Many mobile users receive in excess of 20 text messages a day. If your text message has an element of surprise (although, in accordance to rule number one, it must be an invited surprise) then the viral marketing potential can be realized.

25. *Have fun.* Humour is infectious. And as text messaging is a personal and 'warm' form of media, a sense of fun can prove useful in humanizing your message.

26. *Be honest.* It is true it can be an uphill struggle to gain text message subscribers, but if you have misled them in any way they will realize it eventually. If the big print gives and the small print takes away, your target customers are likely to be unforgiving.

27. *Learn from the SMS success stories.* Look at the SMS services which have taken off in a big way, such as New York Celebrity Sightings, the *Men's Health* Belly Off Club, Tubehell, Pepsi's 'Text to the Max' campaign, and Bridget Jones' Text Diary. Sometimes this success is partly attributable to a strong brand offline, in other cases it is purely the result of word of mouth (or word of text.)

28. *Use the mobile as a back channel.* 'Effectively SMS can turn traditional broadcast advertising into an interactive medium using the mobile phone as the back channel,' says Eamon Hession, a founding member of the Irish Wireless Marketing

Association and Managing Director of Puca. Using the mobile as a back channel also means that you can avoid the spam problem altogether.

29. *Make it easy to subscribe.* Many of the most successful campaigns require users to do little more than send a keyword to a text message number in order to add themselves to the database.

30. *Offer an instant incentive.* As people do not always perceive long-term value, an instant incentive at the point of registration is required. This can be in the form of a free download (of a game, ringtone or logo) or automatic entry into a competition.

31. *Collect information from your subscribers.* Obviously, if the subscription process requires little more than sending a keyword, further information may be required post-registration. 'Start collecting information on the database by sending our interactive survey questions,' advises Eamon Hession. Again, such market research will need to be incentive-based.

32. *Make it easy to unsubscribe.* Users must be able to opt out of any campaign with ease, otherwise you could be accused of sending spam and could jeopardize the relevancy of your database. Furthermore, clear opt-out instructions will help to alleviate subscriber concern at the initial registration process.

33. *Set goals.* These should not simply dictate what you want to achieve, but also how you are going to exceed customer expectations.

34. *Make messages do something.* The easiest way to add value to messages is to turn them into something else, such as a ticket or a coupon.

35. *Follow teen trends.* According to Jupiter analyst Noah Yasskin, 'today's teen behaviour will be mainstream tomorrow'. This has been proved in the case of SMS and instant messenger applications to name but two.

36. *Build infobrands.* 'Developing campaigns that blur the boundaries of promotion and information provision will do very well in the long term, especially for marketers keen to use mobiles as a CRM tool,' says Brainstorm CEO and MMA Chairman Steve Wunker.

37. *Acknowledge user messages.* Research from Enpocket shows that an enticement to enter a draw by replying to SMS is

valued for more if it is followed by an SMS in return acknowledging receipt of the entry.

38. *Maximize the chances for ongoing communication.* For instance, if you are running a competition you could turn it into a multi-level quiz in order to keep the SMS traffic travelling in both directions.

39. *Get in with the operators.* The operators are the intermediaries between you and your customers. As Enpocket's Jeremy Wright put it, 'They hold all the keys: demographics, location, phone message, phone types and reach. And they have the customer relationships, so it is in their best interests to ensure that the audience you seek to reach appreciates the campaign or they could face damaging customer churn.'

40. *Avoid unscrupulous list brokers.* Some companies have a very loose definition of the term 'opt-in' list. Although it is advisable to compile your own list, if you are purchasing one ensure that it is from a media owner which has total responsibility for its customer base. Also, make sure every member of that list is willing to receive promotions from companies other than the list vendor.

41. *Watch Japan.* The combination of i-Mode technology and one of the most innovative network operators on the planet, NTT DoCoMo, means that Japan is at the forefront of the mobile marketing revolution.

42. *Don't underestimate the mobile Internet.* Although it has been a bumpy ride, investment in 3G technology means that the words 'usability' and 'wireless Web' will be able to fit together in the near future.

43. *Don't underestimate SMS.* Some analysts have equated advancements in technology with the eventual demise of SMS. However, these advancements will improve SMS technology as well.

44. *Don't bank on techno prophets.* The people who wrote about the death of SMS do not have a track record of successful future gazing. Consider these former techno prophecies. SMS will never happen. The Y2K bug will wipe out the entire global computer system. WAP 1.0 will be the future of m-commerce. Analysts concentrating on technology alone inevitably get it wrong.

45. *Decide for yourself.* As the various opinions expressed in this

book attest, there is not one answer. Ultimately, it will be up to you to decide what works for your own audience.

46. *Identify your audience.* Who is each message for? Are you creating a message for a clearly defined niche audience or a broad cross-section of mobile users? Is it an international, national or local audience that you are targeting? The answers to these questions will help determine the structure and content of your campaign. The more specific the target audience, the more you will be able to fine-tune the information arriving on your subscriber's mobile devices.

47. *Be clear.* The nature of text messaging, and even WAP, means that you haven't got all day to get your message across. The best advice is to follow the BLUF rule – get the Bottom Line Up Front.

48. *Get the timing right.* Timing is not only the secret of comedy, but also the key to successful mobile marketing. Think of the best time of day, week or month to send out messages. *Men's Health* magazine sent out SMS lunchtime menus between 10.30 and 11.30 in the morning, just as people are starting to plan what to have to eat. *Top of the Pops* magazine sent out messages during the *Top of the Pops* television show. There is always a good time and a bad time for every message.

49. *Use text messaging at events.* Text messaging can be used in a variety of ways to make 'real world' events interactive. For instance, at the UK's Online Music Awards, leading music industry figures are able to vote on the Music Site of the Year award by sending a text message at an allocated time slot. 'By using the audience vote, the OMA is guaranteeing interest in the awards throughout the evening; not an easy task to achieve,' says 12Snap's Anne de Kerckhove.

50. *Think of location.* Combining the right time with the right locations can double your marketing power. For instance, an SMS alert providing a coupon for a can of Red Bull could be effective sent at 10pm. It would be twice as effective if it was sent at that time to a mobile user who had just entered a nightclub. 'Mobile marketing enables brands to increase their level of interaction with customers at the most appropriate time and place to deliver their marketing message,' confirms John Farmer of Carbon Partners.

51. *Use competitions.* Whatever your objectives, competitions

have proved to be a good way of overcoming the first hurdle – getting potential customers to contact you via text.

52. *Promote on products.* Physical products provide the perfect opportunity to promote a campaign. The biggest response ever to a mobile marketing drive came after Cadbury's mentioned their SMS campaign on millions of chocolate bars.

53. *Make campaigns measurable.* If a campaign cannot be measured or audited, it is impossible to gauge success.

54. *Ask questions.* One way to make measuring a campaign easier, as well as to make it more interactive, is to ask your subscribers questions. Moreover, questions indicate that you are a business or brand that is ready and willing to listen to the voice of its customers.

55. *Build trust.* Blatant self-promotion will help you lose trust. In line with the law of diminishing returns, the more your business or brand name is referred to, the more authority over your audience you lose.

56. *Don't over-send.* According to an NOP survey, mobile users are not prepared to receive more than five commercial messages a day. As more businesses jump on the mobile bandwagon, the threat of 'text overload' becomes very real. Don't contribute to the problem by over-sending to your opt-in subscribers.

57. *Respect privacy.* If you are collecting phone numbers or other personal information, be explicit about the fact that you will not sell or pass on these details to other companies.

58. *Be obvious.* Always make it obvious why you are sending a message.

59. *Be legal.* Keep up to date with new data and communications legislation as it emerges.

60. *Get involved with the industry.* Our actions now will determine the future of mobile marketing. By getting involved with industry bodies such as the Mobile Marketing Association it is possible to take a collective stance against spam and other forms of bad practice.

61. *Avoid BS.* Ernest Hemingway famously remarked that all good writers have a 'built-in bulls*** detector'. This is a trait they share with mobile phone users.

62. *Bridge the response gap.* In traditional marketing media, even a 'call to action' can prove ineffective. As a result consumers all too often fall into a response gap between when they see the

message and when they respond. By including a response code in your offline or online marketing, customers can send the response using SMS to request more information or even buy products.

63. *Provide real-time information.* Real-time information services have proved attractive to both WAP and SMS users. Real-time share trading information and sports results have proved particularly successful.

64. *Move into mainstream markets.* The teens may remain the mobile pioneers, but companies have found increasing success targeting older mobile users. 'Having initially appealed as a cheap and handy communication tool for youngsters, text messaging is now being rapidly adopted by the adult community,' confirms Paul Collins, an advisor at new media specialists A T Kearney. In 2001, Channel 4 and Deutsche Bank subsidiary BWS were two of the first companies to reach out to the rising tide of 'silver texters' (the average BWS customer is over 50).

65. *Don't be scared of the 'W' word.* The GPRS version of WAP can't walk your dog, but it can help marketers provide useful information-based services.

66. *If you've got nothing to say, say nothing.* If a text message doesn't have some value to the recipient, don't send it.

67. *Become addictive.* Text messaging is already addictive, and the mobile Internet could be soon. By making sure people look forward to receiving it, your mobile service could be too. The trick is to provide a service which can keep adding value, even in the long term.

68. *Have a sense of humour.* Text is fun, as the number of request-a-joke services testify. Lighten up and share a giggle with your customers. (This principle does not usually apply to chartered accountants or funeral directors.)

69. *Beware of the 'hype cycle'.* The Gartner Consultancy has coined the term 'hype cycle' in order to describe the way in which new technologies are boosted and then slain. Bluetooth, WAP, m-commerce – all have been victims.

70. *Don't wait for the next generation.* Waiting for 3G has been likened to *Waiting for Godot.* Only it has taken a little longer. Who will be bothered to wait for 4G?

71. *Turn your message into your product.* Premium services and reverse-billing enable you to convert your marketing message

into a product itself. But remember, mobile users only pay for tangible value.

72. *Get people voting.* SMS voting has proved excessively popular so far, particularly in the case of reality television shows and award ceremonies. The BAFTA awards and the Brits both enable voters to cast text votes. Mobile operator One2One believes that people will eventually be able to vote in general elections via SMS. A British Market Research Bureau International poll found that 44 per cent of 18 to 24-year-old non-voters would be willing to vote if they could do it via their mobiles. All the main UK operators, and many elsewhere in Europe, also offer voting services.

73. *Acknowledge a phone's full potential.* A mobile 'phone' can now incorporate MP3, radio and various other technologies. In the future, there will be little a phone can't do.

74. *Provide instant information.* Text messaging and the Internet provide users with instant access to information. You therefore need to be able to deliver content as users require it.

75. *The mobile Internet is a four letter word.* GPRS, to be precise. This is the technology that is starting to help WAP-enabled phones deliver a user-friendly experience. The WAP 'brand' may still have to go, though, as GPRS becomes the new buzz acronym.

76. *Exploit the PR potential.* Text messaging and the mobile Internet are both subjects which seem to excite news and feature editors across the globe. By providing a unique element to your service you may be able to add a 'media hook, for editors to bite. New York Celebrity Sightings and the *Guardian's* SMS Poetry Competition both managed to gain international coverage, to name but two. There is another way SMS can help press relations: it can also be used to keep key journalists and editors informed of relevant product and brand news.

77. *Build loyalty.* 'In the future we will see a big move towards mobile marketers developing marketing applications which help build brand loyalty by providing a valuable service to consumers,' predicts MMA Chairman Steve Wunker. For instance, supermarkets can use mobile media to inform shoppers how many loyalty card points they have.

78. *Don't believe the m-commerce hype.* M-commerce transactions are already happening. However, reverse billing and

premium services will still be the main way to drive immediate revenues via mobile marketing campaigns for a while to come.

79. *Think CRM.* Mobile marketing has most value in building and managing long-term customer relations, not short-term sales promotion opportunities.

80. *Generate awareness.* Brand recall rates for SMS campaigns average around the 50 per cent mark, way higher than can be expected online.

81. *Entertain.* Marketers may have to become 'entertainment providers' if they are to adapt fully to the growth in mobile entertainment consoles. To have a head start, look at what's going on in Singapore. As Steve Frank, General Manager at Riot Entertainment Asia has observed, 'Singapore is really leading the way when it comes to wireless entertainment'.

82. *Make customers compete.* Interactive competitions and quizzes have proved themselves as successful ways to build a database up from scratch. The US-based SMS-based trivia game, the Intelligent Quotient Quiz (IQQ) has generated 2 million messages in a one-month period.

83. *Be cool.* Phones are now indispensable fashion accessories and text messaging has become the signifier of an active social life.

84. *Get gaming.* By 2006 there will be 53 million gamers worldwide. 60 per cent of these will be distributed between the Asia-Pacific and Europe. Wireless gaming is expected to be a billion dollar market by 2004, rising to $4.3 billion by 2006. In Europe the real mobile gaming successes that have so far taken off are simple quiz games, such as Who Wants to be a Millionaire?, and Trivial Pursuit. 'Games have to be easy to play and easy to pay,' says Matt Hamalained, Chief Operating Officer at CodeOnline.

85. *Let text lead your marketing activity.* 'Text messaging will have a very positive impact. It will no longer be an add-on service but will lead the way,' predicts Emap's Digital Sales Director Jane Henley.

86. *Get visual.* As multimedia messaging becomes popular, marketers will have to attract users in visual, as well as textual, ways.

87. *Listen to what customers say.* 'The enthusiasm among marketers for developing new ways of pushing information

at consumers has not been matched by an enthusiasm to listen to what consumers say,' argues Mark Curtis, a partner at relationship consultancy Fjord.

88. *Support existing marketing campaigns.* Mobile marketing campaigns should not exist in a 'black hole'.

89. *Outsource where necessary.* Very few companies are able to do everything themselves, given the technical expertise and software solutions required. Database management can be a particularly Herculean task.

90. *Make contact easy.* Mobile marketing is a two-way activity. As such, it is important that consumers can always make instantaneous contact once a message has been sent. This can be via text messaging, e-mail or voice call. Ideally, you should provide the choice. A 'hit call' option within an SMS message is especially effective.

91. *Divide your database.* It is unlikely that all your messages will be relevant to every subscriber. Divide your database into relevant groups in order to guarantee high efficiency and minimize marketing 'wastage'.

92. *Encourage creativity.* Given mobile marketing's two-way nature, campaigns should not only be creative but also encourage creativity. For instance, ice cream makers Ben and Jerry's invited subscribers to 'tell a funky funny story' in return for the chance to win a year's supply of free ice cream.

93. *Offer vouchers.* One of the most obvious ways to make your message do something is to turn it into a voucher or coupon. This also helps you to measure a campaign's response rate directly as well as generate new contacts.

94. *Offer something for free.* Freebies work well providing they are relevant. Free beer often seems to do the trick.

95. *Observe the unique nature of the medium.* As ClickZ columnist Nancy Whiteman has noted, 'wireless is not the Web without wires'.

96. *Embrace action marketing.* Immediate action of some kind must be possible, whether this means saving a coupon, making contact, or even a transaction.

97. *Make messages have a purpose.* Messages need a *raison d'être*. People don't 'surf' or 'browse' via their mobile devices, even when they are accessing the Internet. They normally have a practical and specific purpose for using them. Bland, catch-all

campaigns may build brand awareness on television but they won't cut the mustard with mobile.

98. *Adopt a successful pulling technique.* No, I'm not talking chat-up lines. Users need to be in control of the mobile marketing experience. They want to pull information and services towards them rather than have it pushed in their way.

99. *Avoid interruptive advertising.* Ideally, subscribers should know when you are contacting them, as well as why. As the example of the standard Internet has shown, interruptive advertising doesn't work.

100. *Make it easy.* Usability is everything.

Key organizations

3GPP (The Third Generation Partnership Project)
A body set up to coordinate the development of globally accepted standards for 3G.
ARIB (Association of Radio Industries and Businesses)
The main Japanese telecoms body.
Direct Marketing Association (DMA)
The UK's Direct Marketing Association has a key role to play in raising awareness of the mobile marketing opportunities.
ETSI (European Telecommunications Standards Institute)
European telecoms organization.
GSM Association
The main industry body promoting the GSM standard worldwide.
ITU (International Telecommunications Union)
An international organization responsible for coordinating global telecommunications activities, especially in the area of standards.
MMA (Mobile Marketing Association)
Industry consortium formed from the merger of the US-based Wireless Advertising Association and the UK-based Wireless Marketing Association in January 2002.
Mobile Games Interoperability Forum
Building on the 'Universal Mobile Games Platform' initiative launched in March 2001 by Ericsson, Motorola and Siemens IC Mobile, the Mobile Games Interoperability (MGI) Forum adds Finland's Nokia to the mix. The members are working as a specification to enable game developers to produce and deploy mobile

games across multiple game servers and wireless networks, and enable them to be played over different mobile devices.

TIA (Telecommunications Industry Association)
The US telecoms standards body.

TMForum
The Telecommunications Management Forum, an industry body working to encourage and develop global standards for telecoms management systems.

UMTS Forum
Another 3G organization.

WAP Forum
The industry body created to give substance to WAP protocols. It now has over 200 full-time members who pay substantial fees to belong.

Useful Web sites

Centrifugal Forces: www.centrifugalforces.co.uk
Andy Wilson's Centrifugal Forces publishes and promotes SMS poetry, and is useful for anyone interested in looking to explore the artistic and creative implications of the medium.
ClickZ: www.clickz.com
Wireless marketing advice from a US perspective.
GSM World: www.gsmworld.com
The Web site of the GSM Association includes the latest mobile technology and industry news.
Internet Works: www.iwks.com
As a contributor I may be biased, but Internet Works provides excellent advice on the Internet (fixed and mobile) for small-to-medium businesses.
M for Mobile: www.mformobile.com
A comprehensive source of mobile industry news, views and statistics.
Mobile Gaming Interoperability Forum: www.gsacom.com
The Mobile Gaming Interoperability Forum has been established by key players in the mobile and games industries, to establish a common set of gaming standard across different platforms.
News Now: www.newsnow.co.uk
With updates every five minutes, this has to be one of the best sites for new media news from around the globe. There are pages for both 'Wireless' and 'WAP'.
Simply Wireless.com: www.simplywireless.com
Simply Wireless.com's text messaging centre is packed with useful, if basic, SMS advice.

SMS Shortcuts: www.smsshortcuts.co.za
This African site provides abbreviations for the most common SMS abbreviations.
The Street: www.thestreet.com
The Street's Wireless Wiz column provides authoritative comment on leading developments within the wireless world.
UMTS Forum: www.umts-forum.org
A source of news on the latest 3G developments.
WAP Forum: www.wapforum.org
WAP was developed by the WAP Forum, an industry organization whose primary goal is to bring together companies from different segments of the wireless market. WAP Forum members constitute more than 95 per cent of the global handset market.
WAP Insight: www.wapinsight.com
An online newsletter dedicated to all aspects of WAP.
Wired: www.wired.com
Despite its title, the Web site of the groundbreaking technology magazine is one of the leading sources of information on the use of wireless technology around the world.

Glossary

2G Second generation technology. A term used to describe GSM digital networks.

2.5G Technological upgrades to standard GSM mobile networks which increase data transmission speeds and efficiency. The term encompasses GPRS and EDGE. Viewed as a stepping stone to 3G.

3G 3G technology refers to the third generation of mobile communications after analogue (IG) and digital (2G). While 2G allows for SMS, the mobile Internet and mobile shopping, 3G enables high-quality still pictures, video clips and live video feeds to be sent and managed via mobile phones. This is possible due to a high data transmission rate of 2 megabits per second. Increased bandwidth means mobile television, banking and Web surfing can become as simple as sending a text message.

ADSL Asymmetric digital subscriber line. A high speed, high bandwidth (see below) telephone line.

application server Application servers are often referred to as 'next generation servers' as they excel at running the programming languages that help Web sites and WAP sites to deliver dynamic information like the latest news headlines, stock quotes, personalized information or 'shopping carts'.

attachment A file added to a message to be sent via MMS (the multimedia messaging service).

autoresponders Autoresponders are e-mail and SMS software applications that enable users to send automated messages when they are not able to respond to incoming traffic. Some autoresponse software enables a degree of personalization, for instance by incorporating the recipient's name in the responding message.

average subscriber base   Average number of subscribers.

back-up   A copy of data saved on your computer's hard drive. By making back-ups of your computer's files and programs you can safeguard your data against the threat posed by viruses.

bandwidth   The capacity of fibre optic cables which carry information over networks. The higher the bandwidth, the faster information will pass through a cable, and therefore the faster information can be downloaded or uploaded via the Internet.

banner ad   An electronic advertisement displayed as a band of text and graphics within a Web or WAP page. The fact that many Internet users can now set their browsers to ignore banner ads has led to advertisers looking for other types of online advertising.

Bluetooth   A communications specification designed to enable mobile phones, computer, and other devices to share information and synchronize data. This technology requires a special Bluetooth chip in each device.

broadband   High bandwidth technology which is revolutionizing the way mobile technology is used by businesses and consumers.

brochureware   A derogatory term used to describe commercial text message and Web content that resembles a company brochure. Brochureware messages depend (like their printed counterparts) on one-way not two-way communication.

CDMA   Code Division Multiple Access. A technology for digital transmission of radio signals between, for example, a mobile telephone and a radio base station. In CDMA, a frequency is divided using codes, rather than in time or through frequency separation.

character set   The sets of characters needed to display text in various languages. For example, in order to view Japanese characters, you need to have the Japanese character set.

chat   Chat systems enable SMS and Internet users to communicate in real time. Messages posted via a chat system will be seen by every member of the participating group.

cHTML   Compact HTML, the markup language employed by NTT DoCoMo for sites on its i-Mode service, the arch rival to WAP.

churn   In the United Kingdom, Orange defines churn as the number of subscribers who are disconnected from its network, excluding those who disconnect pursuant to Orange's 14-day money back guarantee.

click through   When someone clicks on a message to get something else.

community   A group of Internet or mobile users with a shared interest or loyalty who interact with each other via their devices.

contact list   A collection of text message numbers or e-mail addresses of people who have asked to receive messages.

contact list manager   An automated program to handle the administrative functions of adding and removing subscribers.

content   The textual, graphical and multimedia material that constitutes a text message or WAP page.

content management   The means and methods of managing the textual and graphical content for a campaign.

conversion rate   The percentage of subscribers who turn into customers.

cross-posting   The act of posting the same messages to several different groups of subscribers simultaneously.

customizable covers   Users can now change the front cover of their mobile phone and replace it with a different coloured or patterned cover at any time.

cyberspace   Term originally coined in the sci-fi novels of William Gibson, referring to the online world and its communication networks, evoking its intangible sense of space. The first time the word was used was in Gibson's novel *Neuromancer*: 'Cyberspace. A consensual hallucination experienced daily by billions of legitimate operators... A graphic representation of data abstracted from the banks of every computer in the human system.'

domain name   The officially registered address of a Web site or WAP site. Domain names typically contain two or more parts separated by a dot.

downloadable ringtones   The possibility of transferring a melody from the Internet via SMS to install it as the ringing tone on a mobile phone.

EASY MESSAGE T9™   Predictive and intuitive software to simplify and speed up entry of short messages (SMS).

EDGE   Enhanced data rates for global evolution. EDGE is a technology that gives network standards such as GSM and TDMA similar capacity to handle services for 3G.

e-mail   Electronic mail. A message sent across the Internet, or the act of transferring messages between mobile phones or other communications devices attached to the Internet.

EMS   Enhanced messaging services. An enhancement of SMS, in that it supports black and white pictures and animation formats.

emoticons   Common symbols used in text messages to denote particular emotions by resembling faces on their side. :-) therefore indicates happiness (a smiley face). The word 'emoticon' combines 'emotion' with 'icon'. Emoticons are commonly referred to as 'smileys'.

encryption   A method used to secure data that is transferred over the Internet by scrambling it in such a way that only the intended recipient of the message can read its contents.

filter   Software that can discriminate between types of incoming and ongoing text messages or e-mails.

flame   A hostile or aggressive message sent via e-mail or text. Typically, flame messages are sent in response to spam or unsolicited commercial messages.

forward   To send a copy to a message to another number or address. Forwarding is usually done when you want to share a message you have received with someone else.

GIF   Short for graphic information file. Used on the Internet and MMS to display files that contain graphic images.

GPRS   The GPRS (General Packet Radio Service) is an extension of the GSM network enabling the transmission of data 'packets' at high speeds, like the Internet. With speeds up to 10 times higher than GSM, the network provides virtually instant and permanent connections.

graphic display   High definition display unit to display and animate icons.

groupware   A set of technology tools enabling businesses to share software.

GSM   GSM stands for 'Global System for Mobile Communications'. It is a worldwide digital mobile phone standard. GSM phones can therefore be used in many countries around the world, in particular in continental Europe, the Middle East, and Asia Pacific. It is not used, however, in Japan or the United States.

HDML   Handheld Device Markup Language. A language that formats information for mobile phones or handheld computers in the same way that HTML does for PCs. It was the predecessor to WML (Wireless Markup Language).

HTML   Hypertext Mark-up Language. A computer code used to build and develop Web pages. It is used to format the text of a document, indicate hyperlinks to other Web pages and describe the layout of the Web page. WAP sites cannot be built with HTML, which means WAP developers have had to rewrite their Web sites from scratch.

hyperlink   Most commonly found on Web and WAP pages, hyperlinks are either images or pieces of text which, when a user clicks on them, enable users to 'click through' to other pages. They can be used to connect internally, to connect to Web pages within the same site, as well as externally, to link to other Web sites. Hyperlinks can be added to Web pages by using simple HTML commands. They can also be used in e-mail messages, for example to include the address of a company's Web site. Also referred to as a hypertext link.

i-Mode   Information mode. A play on the Japanese word for anywhere, i-Mode is similar to WAP but owned by NTT DoCoMo at present. It uses cHTML (compact HTML) as its markup language instead of WML like WAP.

IMSI   International mobile subscriber identity. The number normally inscribed on a GSM handset to identify it. Dual-IMSI is also possible.

IMT 2000   International Mobile Telecommunications 2000. The ITU's standard for 3G mobile networks. Intended to provide a global framework for intelligent mobile data networks. UMTS (Universal Mobile Telecommunications System) is Europe's proposal for IMT 2000.

infomediary   A company or service that provides and aggregates relevant customer or industry information.

ISDN   Integrated Services Digital Network. The standard developed by the ITU (International Telecommunications Union) for digital telephone networks on which GSM is heavily based. Indeed when you make a data connection over GSM it is in fact an ISDN call slowed down.

itchy thumb syndrome   A slang reference to the Internet user's hunger for interactivity. Sites can combat this 'syndrome' by adding interactive elements such as hyperlinks and online forums.

junk text   See 'spam'.

killer app   The term 'killer app' became popularized with the publication of *Unleashing the Killer App* by Larry Downes and Chunka Mui in 1998. The authors define a killer app as 'a new good or service that establishes an entirely new category and, by being first, dominates it, returning several hundred per cent on the initial investment. Killer apps are the Holy Grail of technology investors, the stuff of which their silicon dreams are made'. Text messaging and the Web are two examples of 'killer apps'.

m-business The catch-all term referring to the mobile business world. It also signifies an individual online business or company.

m-commerce Online commercial activity conducted via the mobile Internet, using mobile phones and other wireless devices. Leading Internet figures such as Jeff Bezos, founder of Amazon, and David Potter, Chairman of Psion, predict that m-commerce will soon eclipse commerce conducted via desktop computers.

Metcalfe's law Robert Metcalfe, founder of 3Com, found that networks dramatically increase in value with each additional user. Metcalfe's Law has therefore been instrumental to the concept of viral marketing.

micro-browser Client software designed to overcome challenges of mobile handheld devices that enables wireless access to services such as Internet information in combination with a suitable network server.

MP3 A compressed digital format for audio files. Users can now listen to music downloaded from the Internet directly on their mobile phone.

MSC Mobile Switching Centre: a switch providing services and coordination between mobile users in a mobile network and external networks.

m-tailing The selling of retail goods via mobile devices.

newbie Slang term for a new text message user.

niche A narrow but unified market or audience segment. The mobile medium is particularly suited to niche markets and audiences.

PDA Personal Digital Assistant, which has advanced features such as an agenda, word processing and spreadsheet. Fitted with a wide screen, data entry is via a keyboard or a stylus (on a touch pad). A PDA also gives access to the Web and e-mail. PDAs with a built-in WAP/GPRS mobile phone are now available.

PIN (code) Personal identification number. Personal access code from 4 to 8 numbers long allowing use of a SIM card. If the wrong PIN code is entered three times in a row, your card is blocked.

portal A Web site that provides a window or 'doorway' onto the Web or mobile Internet. Search engines and directories are the most common portal sites.

prepay customer A customer who buys air time in advance, by purchasing vouchers from an operator's retail outlet for example.

protocol   The rules for data transferred over mobile networks so that devices understand what to do when they receive the information.

pull   A 'pull' medium is one which users pull information towards them rather than have it pushed in their direction.

pull technology   The Internet and text messaging are essentially 'pull' technologies. Understanding the 'pull' nature of the mobile Internet is often considered to be one of the key factors in determining a campaign's success.

real world   Everything outside the Internet.

redirect   A way to send a message that you have received to someone else.

response management   A mobile marketing term referring to the process of managing responses or leads from the time they are received through conversion to sale.

ringtones   Ringtones are one of the major growth mobile industries, and mobile users can use their mobile phones to compose a melody or download one from the Internet.

roaming   Technical name for the ability of a single handset to work in conjunction with more than one mobile network. In practice roaming means that the handset will work when its owner travels abroad.

SCS   Sales and service companies (sociétés de commercialization et de services). These companies manage subscriptions to mobile and fixed telephone networks and serve as intermediaries between operators and sellers or subscribers.

secure message   A text or e-mail message that has been encoded or encrypted (eg with a digital signature, to avoid interception).

signature line   A few words placed at the end of a text message to provide the reader with relevant sender contact information.

SIM   Subscriber identity module. A card inserted inside a mobile handset to provide all pertinent information about the user including airtime creditworthiness. Created to prevent airtime frauds, it has now been adapted so that it is possible to run a WAP browser on a SIM card.

smiley   See 'emoticon'.

SMS   Short messaging service. The ability to send and receive text messages to and from mobile telephones. The text can be words or numbers or a combination of both. SMS was created when it was incorporated into the Global System for Mobiles (GSM) digital mobile phone standard. A single short message can be up to 160 characters of text in length using default GSM alphabet coding.

SMS centre   SMS is a store-and-forward technology. A sent SMS will be stored at an SMS centre until the receiver's phone is switched on to receive it.

SMTP   Simple Mail Transport Protocol. An e-mail interface enabling users to send short text messages.

snail mail   Derogative reference for the offline postal service, which is viewed as slow in comparison to electronic mail and text messaging.

snooze news   Product 'news' which will not interest mobile users.

spam   Unsolicited bulk text messages, usually sent for commercial purposes. Spam is used by some companies as a cheap form of advertising, although it is generally considered offensive and unwelcome by the mobile community. Spamming is considered unethical because it is intrusive and eats up phone memory. Various industry bodies, such as the Mobile Marketing Association, campaign actively against spam and those individuals or organizations accused of spamming. The term originates from the Monty Python sketch in which customers at a 'greasy spoon' café are served spam with everything regardless of whether it was part of their order. Spam also refers to unsolicited commercial messages posted via e-mail.

TDMA   Time Division Multiple Access. An old telephony-based protocol which has now given its name to a type of digital network championed in the United States by Ericsson. It bears a close enough resemblance to GSM that an enhanced version of GPRS (EDGE) will work on both TDMA and GSM networks.

text-head   SMS-obsessed individual.

text message   A short alphanumeric message received via a mobile device.

UCT   Unsolicited commercial text messages. See 'spam'.

UMTS   Universal Mobile Telecommunications System intended mainly for the evolution of GSM networks.

WAP   WAP is the leading global open standard for applications over wireless networks. Just as http (hypertext transfer protocol) – as in the 'http://' prefix for Web addresses - facilitates a system for PCs and laptops to access information from a remote server over various wirelines, WAP does the same for microbrowsers on wireless devices.

WAP gateway   A WAP gateway offers a two-way link which connects a WAP-enabled mobile phone to a traditional Internet (HTTP) server. As a WAP device can only 'understand' information held in WML with its tokenized/compiled/binary format, the function of the WAP gateway is to convert content into an intelligible format. On the HTTP server's side, the WAP gateway can provide additional information about the WAP device through HTTP headers.

WML   Wireless Markup Language. A language developed to control the presentation of Web pages on mobile phones and PDAs in the same way as HTML does for PCs. Part of the Wireless Access Protocol (WAP), WML is an open standard, and is supported by most mobile phones.

XHTML   EXtensible Hyper Text Markup Language. The code needed to bridge the gap between WAP and the fixed Internet (WWW). XHTML merges key elements of Wireless Application Protocol (WAP) and the fixed Web to allow companies to create a single, dynamic interface that can be adapted quickly to multiple types of fixed and mobile browsers.

XML   EXtensible Markup Language. Created as a kind of 'meta language' to create Web sites using a number of different methods. These methods include both WML and HTML.

Index

NB: figures in *italics* indicate figures